Education in Recession

Education in Recession

Crisis in County Hall and Classroom

Eric Hewton

University of Sussex

London
ALLEN & UNWIN
Boston   Sydney

Allen & Unwin (Publishers) Ltd,
40 Museum Street, London WC1A 1LU, UK

Allen & Unwin (Publishers) Ltd,
Park Lane, Hemel Hempstead, Herts HP2 4TE, UK

Allen & Unwin, Inc.,
8 Winchester Place, Winchester, Mass. 01890, USA

Allen & Unwin (Australia) Ltd,
8 Napier Street, North Sydney, NSW 2060, Australia

First published in 1986

British Library Cataloguing in Publication Data

Hewton, Eric
    Education in recession: crisis in county hall and the classroom.
    1. Education – Great Britain   2. Depressions
    3. Great Britain – Economic conditions – 1945–
I. Title
370′.941   LA637.7
ISBN 0-04-379003-8
ISBN 0-04-379004-6 Pbk

Library of Congress Cataloging-in-Publication Data

Hewton, Eric
    Education in recession.   ESSEX COUNTY LIBRARY
    Bibliography: p.
Includes index.
1. Education – Great Britain – Finance.
2. School closings – Great Britain.   3. Federal aid to   OR 12-7-93
education – Great Britain.   I. Title.
LB2826.6.G7H49   1986   379.1′21′0941   85-18704
ISBN 0-04-379003-8 (alk. paper)
ISBN 0-04-379004-6 (pbk.: alk. paper)

Set in 11 on 12 point Garamond by Paston Press, Norwich
and printed in Great Britain by Biddles Ltd, Guildford, Surrey

ublishers gratefully acknowledge permission to reproduc
m Northern Songs c/o CBS Songs.

To Education?

When I was younger, so much younger than today,
I never needed anybody's help in any way;
But now my life has changed in oh, so many ways,
My independence seems to vanish in the haze . . .
Won't you please, please help me.

(Lennon and McCartney)

Contents

Preface

This study was motivated by several factors: my own personal and teaching interest in organizations and how they function; my previous research in the economics of education and present participation in an organization itself undergoing the process of financial contraction; my past connections with one local authority currently engaged in cost-cutting exercises; and finally, but most importantly, a growing concern with the effects of the cuts on the educational system.

I wanted to know more about how a complex organization like a local authority set about dealing with the problem of contraction. I also wanted to know whether there were any general principles and difficulties involved that might apply to other organizations in this situation. With these interests in mind I approached a local authority (which, for reasons explained on p. 10, will be called a 'shire') where I had done some earlier work and senior officers agreed to co-operate in a project which I called at the time 'Policy-Making in a Local Education Authority in a Time of Contraction'.

I also approached the Nuffield Foundation for a grant, to cover mainly travel and subsistence expenses, under their Social Sciences Small Grants Scheme. This was awarded in 1981, and it is worth noting some of the points made in that application for they indicate 'where I went in' and can be compared with the conclusions 'I came out with'. The following is a brief extract from my original application:

> Most Local Education Authorities are having to reduce expenditure – some by 10% or more. This contrasts with the situation a few years ago when most were geared to growth. The procedures which were found appropriate and acceptable for allocating resources during a period of expansion may no longer be feasible. Councils are having to find ways

of imposing cuts on their own departments and their activities.

The key research question is: how does a complex organization (in this case a local authority and, in particular, an education department within it) curtail its activities in order to reduce expenditure?

The research falls within the general area of 'policy analysis' but it has a specific focus which is provided by two sub-questions: first, is there a difference in policy making in times of contraction compared with periods of stability and growth; and secondly, are techniques of rational planning, budgeting and policy making (e.g. PPBS) applicable in times of contraction?

From what I have observed during my preliminary work . . . it seems that contraction is not the direct reverse of growth. What goes up does not come down in the same way: new factors enter into the process . . .

It is possible that organizational decline, as opposed to growth, may become a more prevalent feature of society and that organizations will have to adjust their structures and procedures to allow for this. The research should be of help in indicating the barriers which hinder effective decision making in such circumstances.

One of the main findings of my work was that indeed local authorities are changing and that they now operate in very different ways to the growth period of over a decade ago. This is one of the themes of the book. I also found in connection with this that the change was affecting individuals and groups in quite a profound way.

Put simply, and I will elaborate much more on this in later chapters, many people feel themselves in a 'catch 22' position. The alternatives open to them all carry risks and penalties. One option is to 'fight the cuts' and resist all intrusions into their professional or political domain. These are the defenders. A hopeless cause? Some think so, others do not. A second option is to think forward and think big. So education is under attack and many of its traditional values and procedures are being questioned – perhaps this is the time for radical change whilst the door is ajar! These are the reformers. But is their cause any more feasible or worthwhile than that of the defenders? Finally there are the pragmatists, those who reluctantly make the best of a bad job. Feeling very unhappy, they make cuts but try to avoid as much damage as they can.

People vacillate between the three positions. So do groups. So do I. A reflective statement might at this stage prove useful, not merely to express my own values but also to typify the dilemma faced by individuals and groups in local government required to start dismantling what they have for so long sought to build up.

Soliloquy

In principle I detest what is happening to local government and the services which it provides – especially education. Most of my career has been spent in education either teaching or researching. My attitudes were formed during a period of growth, and education, for me, became as much a consumer good as a form of investment. As a society, we should provide as much education as individuals want and should attempt to offer equal access and opportunities.

The cuts move us away from this ideal. There are less resources and fewer opportunities. Education is increasingly regarded as a prelude to employment, assuming that such can be found by young people, rather than as a means to personal growth.

My values apply as much to higher education, where I work, as to the schools I have looked at. Like those who work in the schools, I have had to face unwanted cuts and have demonstrated against them. But I have reluctantly adopted the role of pragmatist. At least I still have a job, I say to myself, and perhaps there was, indeed, some room to trim back a little and become more efficient! The deterioration of the staff–student ratio in my department from 1:8.5 to 1:14 indicates that this form of 'productivity' increase is possible.

What of the future if the cuts continue? Herein lies my greatest fear. The real defender would not tolerate such massive external interference. There would be no compromise; each small battle would be fought until irretrievably lost, and admission of defeat would not, even then, come easily. Pragmatism would be derided as a weak coping mechanism, and forced compliance would be the only retreat. 'Hang on until the government and the times change' would be the rallying call.

My acceptance of the cuts imposed so far involves me in a form of complicity with those who seek the cuts. My actions may possibly save my job and help to preserve the jobs of my colleagues in the short term, but they will destroy ideals that have been worked for by past generations and build up problems for those yet to come. By acting pragmatically I have helped to burn our collective boats. Those who imposed the cuts have proved their point. 'You see, it can be done for less', they can now say.

To imagine a future in which ever more radical changes are contemplated – surely that is no less than treason against the defenders' cause. Even to suggest the possibility of alternatives which may, possibly, be more appropriate and efficient is to break ranks and to provide the opportunity for the enemy to penetrate and destroy.

But against this I have some opposing feelings. Some of the ideals I strove for have not been achieved and this despite abundance of money when it was needed. Simply putting more money into the system does not guarantee better results. Some rethinking of priorities and methods is, surely, necessary. Furthermore, I am not convinced that a new government would reverse the current trend. Any other party coming to power would probably have more important immediate priorities than education. Even if it did put education high upon its list, several more years of cuts are still probable, and this can only make matters worse.

Thinking now like a reformist I can despise the pragmatist in myself almost as much as the defenders do. The pragmatic solution is to cut at the weakest points. What will remain eventually are services denuded of vitality; merely skeletons retaining their shape but offering no excitement nor hope for the future. Perhaps the whole thing does have to be looked at again. Perhaps professional practice in education does have to be examined carefully. But *no*, says the defender in me, that is not what I want to do. And so the dilemma persists.

From this position, and with this experience, I talked to a lot of people, particularly officers, councillors and teachers, all of whom agreed to help me despite considerable pressures on their time. To them I give my thanks and admiration.

I would like to thank especially the Chief Executive, the Chief Education Officers (for there were two over the period of my research) and the County Treasurer of 'Shire' County. They sometimes seemed glad to talk to an uninvolved outsider about the extremely difficult situations they were facing, and this made my work all the more worthwhile and enjoyable.

I am also indebted to many other people within local government and elsewhere for helping me come to terms with some of the issues involved. Also to those colleagues who read the manuscript, sometimes more than once, and made so many helpful comments. Tony Becher, as always, was a stalwart and helpful critic.

My thanks also for the good advice given to me by Pat Thomas at the Nuffield Foundation and for the sum of money from that source which made the study possible.

ERIC HEWTON

1

The Cuts

In 1985 the industrial action by teachers began in earnest. The salary negotiations were deadlocked, and there was much bitterness over what teachers regarded as the arbitrary nature of the government's stance on salary restructuring and conditions of service. Morale in schools had reached a new low ebb. There were promises of more money for education overall if teachers agreed to major reforms but at first there was no definite figure put on this. All indications suggested that it would be a relatively small sum in any case. The National Union of Teachers (the largest of the teaching unions) withdrew from formal negotiations, and a number of measures, including a ban on meetings and lunchtime supervision duties, backed up by selective strike action, began early in 1985. Other unions and professional associations (but not all) added to the disruption with measures designed to disturb but not prevent the operation of schools.

The problem, it seemed, was caused by the inadequate amount of money available to pay teachers and provide the other resources upon which schools relied. The 1985 action by teachers, however, was to a large extent a 'last straw'; it was the result of nearly a decade of cuts – although this clearly depends upon how cuts are defined. This book attempts to analyse the problem of 'education in recession' and to look behind and beyond the 1985 industrial action at the dilemmas faced by local education authorities and their employees in the 1970s and 1980s.

Education in Recession?

'Save Education'; 'Our Children Our Future'; 'Fight the Cuts'. These are the education battle-slogans of the 1980s.

Schools are being starved of resources. The number of books bought by schools per annum fell by 5 million between 1979 and 1981. Schools are understaffed but in 1983 there were 38,000 trained and qualified teachers without teaching posts. One and a half million children are in classes of over thirty-one pupils. Only 20 per cent of children can go to nursery school, and that number is being reduced. So maintains the National Union of Teachers (NUT, 1983).

Around the country, dramatizing these statements, there are demonstrations of all kinds: teachers on strike; teachers refusing to co-operate with their local authority; marches on 'County Hall' or Westminster by parents, teachers and pupils; parents chaining themselves to school railings or blocking main roads to protest against the disappearance of the 'lollipop patrols'; the much-publicized 'march of the dinner ladies' demonstrating against the loss of their jobs.

Anyone involved with providing or supporting education knows about the cuts. It is a regular staff-room topic of conversation. Governors wrestle with difficult staffing problems caused by contraction. Teachers teach in dilapidated buildings. Parent–teacher associations pour money and assistance into the schools – often paying for things that would normally be the responsibility of the local authority. Morale in the teaching profession has reached a new low with very little chance of promotion or movement to other schools. Many teachers over 50 are simply coasting to retirement and can't wait to get out of the profession.

Something is clearly wrong in the educational world. At least this is what the media, the unions and the experience of having children at school in the state system seem to suggest. But then, how is it possible to reconcile this with a statement from the Department of Education and Science (DES, 1983) which reads:

> Total public spending on non-university education in England and university education in Great Britain rose from £11.4 billion in 1981–82 to £12.2 billion in 1982–83 . . . In cost terms (i.e. after allowing for price increases in the economy as a whole) expenditure increased by 1 per cent

between 1978–79 and 1983–84, despite the reduction (of
over 10%) in pupil numbers in the period. *As a result there
was a steady increase in the level of provision for each pupil*
(my emphasis).

(p. 2)

These two 'pictures' simply do not match. There are
obviously political factors at work. The government is
pledged to curb public expenditure but, at the same time, it
is concerned to show that an important service like education
is not suffering. Against this, it is hard for the average teacher
or parent to believe that expenditure is actually increasing
when the schools are begging for materials, classrooms are
not decorated for ten years or more, playing-fields are
neglected, music lessons have to be paid for, subjects are
disappearing from the timetable, schools are closing, and
growing numbers of teachers are taking early retirement.

One explanation is the unusual phenomenon of falling
rolls. In the early and mid-1970s there was a fall-off in the
birth rate. As a result, by the end of the decade, less children
were starting school. This reduction in total numbers of
pupils is gradually working its way through the system. The
government insists that the number of teachers be reduced
correspondingly. In England and Wales in 1979 there were
470,000 teachers. By 1984 there were 439,000 and this
number is projected to fall still further throughout this
decade (DES, 1985, p. 46).

This reduction in teacher numbers underlies 'the cuts' but
it is only part of the story. Alongside is the problem of the
reduction in public expenditure generally and the battle
between central and local government over money. In the
middle of this conflict are the local authorities. The situation
for them is often described as one of crisis.

The authorities provide a number of local services (such as
education, social services, police, roads and fire protection)
of which education is by far the largest spender – usually
taking more than half of the annual budget. For many years
the government paid about two-thirds of the cost of these
services through the rate support grant. In the last decade,

however, it has introduced increasingly strict measures to curb local spending, and the grant has steadily been reduced from over 60 per cent in 1974/5 to about 47 per cent in 1985/6.

This represents a considerable reduction in income for local authorities – in line with government intentions. Furthermore, to prevent them making up the deficit in other ways, constraints such as cash limits, targets, penalties and rate capping have been progressively introduced. To focus attention on potential areas of cost saving, a new body – the Audit Commission for Local Authorities – was set up in 1983 to improve local government economy, efficiency and effectiveness.

The authorities are, therefore, faced with two unpleasant options. They can either disregard government wishes and continue to spend according to their own scale of priorities (thereby risking financial penalties through further reduction in the central grant); or they can attempt to concur with government policy and reduce expenditure on selected services.

Some authorities (such as Liverpool, Lambeth, Sheffield and the Greater London Council) have deliberately defied the government, and their 'fight' has made national news. Others (such as Buckinghamshire, Cambridgeshire, Cornwall, Bury and Wolverhampton, amongst many others) have found their centrally imposed targets so far below their current expenditure that, even with a will to co-operate, reductions of the size required present massive problems.

The saga continues, and many senior officers in local government predict little or no let-up in central government pressure for some years to come.

In theory, these government-required cuts are demanded of each local authority as a whole and need not involve education. In practice, however, this is far from the case. Education cannot escape its share, and possibly more than its share, of the cuts. As Stewart (1983) warned:

The relationship between local authorities and central

government moves towards crisis. Central government has set targets for local authority expenditure which local authorities are neither able nor willing to meet . . .

The education service should appreciate that this is an argument about expenditure on education, as much as it is about local government expenditure in general. All English shire counties except two are alleged to be overspending; nearly two thirds of them by more than 4 per cent. All metropolitan districts except four are alleged to be over-spending, again nearly two thirds of them by 4 per cent. These are education authorities. It is in these authorities that the main overspending is alleged to have taken place . . .

Education accounts for over half the expenditure of these non-conforming shire counties and metropolitan districts. What is being argued about is not an abstraction called local government expenditure, but about actual expenditure on education.

(p. 4)

Education in Recession is the title of this book, but the phrase has more than one meaning. Education is in an economy which is in recession – generally defined by economists as 'a temporary falling off in business activity'. The effects are normally felt by most sectors of the economy through a slowing down in the rate of growth or, more severely, by a period of actual decline. In this sense education is in recession.

Education is also in recession within itself. As already mentioned, numbers entering the education system have fallen. In maintained schools in England and Wales the number of pupils dropped from about 8.5 million in 1976 to just over 7.3 million in 1985. Along with this went reductions in the number of teachers and, nationwide, a pro-gramme of school closures.

There is, however, a third and equally important social–psychological sense in which education is in recession. It has been forced to recede or fall back from its position of pre-eminence amongst the public services which it occupied during the 1950s and 1960s. It was then accorded the status of leader in the fight against social and economic ills of all kinds. It could, it was then argued, pave the way for economic growth, greater social equality, improved living conditions and generally a better organized, stable and satisfied society.

Education no longer has this status. It faces criticism from all sides accompanied by continual calls for greater accountability and better value for money. Its place amongst the privileged professions has receded, and with it has gone its previous, strongly supported claim to increasing amounts of the nation's resources.

A number of questions are raised by the problem of education in recession in the three senses mentioned above.

First, what are the effects of the cuts on the schools themselves? Behind the political statements and slogans, what is it like to teach and learn in the primary and secondary schools of today? Are conditions and morale worse than they were a decade or more ago?

Secondly, what is the role of the local authorities in administering the cuts? They are seemingly caught in the middle between government policies and the needs and demands of the local communities which they serve. They are much criticized by their clients and by the local political opposition. Do they deserve such criticism? Who are the people who make the decisions which affect education? How do they go about the task of ordering priorities? Who has the most influence? Why does education always seem to be the main target for the cuts? Has there been a dramatic change in the way local authorities work in recent years? Do they really face a crisis?

Thirdly, if, as seems likely, the cuts continue, how will this influence the way local authorities operate and make important policy decisions, particularly those which affect education? Are we witnessing a long-term, radical change in the climate of local government: one which will influence time-honoured practices and procedures? Indeed, are we moving towards a 'cuts culture'?

These are the important questions which provide the structure for this book.

The Nature and Structure of the Book

Part I is about the cuts and their effects on the schools. Part II is about the changing cultures of local government and the way in which policy, particularly policy concerning education, is made. Part III looks to the future and speculates on how local authorities will cope in a continuing period of recession.

The answers to the questions posed above are not easily found. The reality behind the politics and polemics is a complex and varied one. What is happening in Sheffield or Inner London may be very different from events in Hampshire or Oxfordshire. But there are similarities. All authorities face the cuts to varying degrees and all have the problem of making difficult choices in a time of recession. They may not make the same decisions, but the processes which lead them to their decisions have much in common across the whole of local government.

To explore the issue of recession and the cuts it is necessary to examine the problem at three levels: the national scene, the local government milieu and the schools themselves. At the national level there is abundant evidence from reports, circulars, White Papers, etc., and a vast amount of critical comment in books and journals. There is also some evidence from similar sources about the plight of local authorities in general.

What is lacking, however, is detailed information about the day-to-day workings of local authorities wrestling with the problem of recession. To provide some evidence of this kind, one local authority, henceforth called Shire, was studied over a period of three years (1981–4). Its schools were visited; its headteachers responded to questionnaires; senior officers and councillors were interviewed; meetings were observed, and internal documents analysed. (More details of the methods used are set out in the Appendix.)

The Shire case study provides the grounding for the analysis which follows. The story is woven from the strands of the three levels – national, local authority and schools –

and moves back and forth between the three using each one to illustrate and explain the others. The chief focus, though, is the local authority and its unenviable 'piggy in the middle' role. The focus is also on the primary and secondary sectors of education. *This is not to deny the problems of further and higher education but simply to single out the largest and, in total financial terms, the most affected area of education.*

The County of Shire

Initially it was felt that anonymity would be useful in order to preserve the sometimes confidential nature of the interviews and documents, but officers of the council who read drafts of the study indicated that they were not concerned about this and that in any case it would not be difficult for the diligent reader to recognize the county from the statistics. It was decided, even so, to retain the thin veil of anonymity to encourage the reader to identify general, rather than specific, issues since what is happening in Shire is representative of changes taking place in many local authorities.

Shire is largely rural but has its city and several large towns which provide an industrial base. In terms of population size it is close to the national average for rural authorities, and the same applies for its annual expenditure, its rates and the number of people employed by the county council.

In a booklet comparing the county with the nation, the Chairman of Council points out that in Shire the rate of population growth, increase in the very elderly, proportion of children in the population, road network to be maintained and proportion of school-leavers among the unemployed are all higher than the national average. As will be seen later, these factors add to the county's problems in a time of contracting resources.

Traditionally Shire has had a Conservative-dominated county council, although experienced members and officers suggest that it was an 'independent' form of conservatism. In the 1981 local elections, however, there was a considerable change in the political balance between the parties, and the Conservatives, aligned with a few Independents, held on to a very slim overall majority. An opposition, formed mainly of Labour and Liberal councillors, emerged and added a new dimension to the policy debate – a situation experienced by many other previously Conservative-dominated authorities.

The name Shire has been adopted in order to refer to a specific, yet typical, county in which the process of recession in education, and its outcomes, can be analysed and interpreted. Why was Shire chosen rather than another authority? Most importantly, senior officers were sympathetic to the study and were prepared to offer time and facilities. Without these the study would not have been feasible. It was also chosen because, despite some special features, it was broadly representative of a large group of authorities under pressure to contract and attempting to comply with central government instructions. This group regarded partnership between central and local government as important and were trying to maintain it in very difficult circumstances.

Like most other authorities, Shire was engaged in reducing its educational expenditure. Between 1976 and 1984 it 'saved' about £10 million, although the exact meaning of 'saved' is examined in detail later. The story which emerges is one which probably holds for most of the thirty-nine local education authorities in the counties and for many of those in the metropolitan districts and parts of London as well.

Organizational structure was another reason for choosing Shire. In the 1970s the county introduced a strong corporate management system and adopted a number of systematic management techniques for planning and financial control. In the 1980s, along with most other non-metropolitan authorities, it was having to face up to 'the cuts'. An important question was, therefore, To what extent would an organizational system created during periods of stability and growth prove useful during times of contraction?

In summary, the essence of the book is recession – both within and around the education system. The cuts have resulted in reductions in educational provision, and the local authorities have been faced with the task of administering the contraction of the service. The study is concerned with the effects upon the schools, the major factors leading to this situation, the changing role of local authorities and the problems they will face in the future if recession continues. We begin with the schools.

2

Recession, Cuts and the Schools

There are two ways of assessing the effects of recession upon the schools. The first is from the outside, using whatever evidence is available to build up a general picture into which a good many individual schools will probably fit. There is, for instance, evidence from national and local sources such as Her Majesty's Inspectorate (HMI) reports, surveys carried out by unions and professional associations, and general feedback from local education authority advisers and other officials who visit the schools. This is often added to by reports in the press and on radio and television. Such evidence helps to create an overall impression of what it is like in the schools.

This impressionistic view often forms the basis for arguments used by pressure groups in reporting, debate and decision-making. General statements and comments, emerging in the first instance from national surveys, eventually become accepted as the norm and are applied to all schools in the same way. Furthermore, what is omitted from such statements is often overlooked altogether. The process can be a dangerous and self-fulfilling one. HMIs and unions may refer to low morale; some councillors may pick up the theme and, suddenly, there is low morale. At least this is the view expressed by some officers and councillors who are suspicious of easily made, broad generalizations. Clearly each issue needs careful consideration in its own context.

Yet the broad view is important. It indicates a general climate in which schools operate and, even if each one differs within it they are likely to be affected by it, directly or indirectly. An analysis of the effects of recession upon schools, therefore, is not complete unless it pays due regard to the broader scene as a backcloth against which to view particular instances.

The second approach to understanding the effects of the cuts is via the schools themselves. Using this approach the researcher tries to establish the issues and concerns experienced and expressed by those within the system. The questions asked are related to how those involved view their situation. What are their thoughts, feelings and actions as they cope with their day-to-day tasks? Perhaps cuts and contraction are uppermost in their minds but perhaps not.

In studying Shire and its schools fifty members of staff of sixteen schools were interviewed on the theme of change generally rather than the cuts *per se*. Out of this came views about the present situation which were sometimes idiosyncratic and sometimes unexpected. As such, they represented the way individuals felt about their job in the current climate. But there also emerged a number of shared concerns which clearly indicated local issues of some importance. Both idiosyncratic and shared concerns provide valuable evidence and generate further useful questions in building up this particular picture.

The sixteen schools visited, despite being carefully chosen to illustrate different kinds of establishment, represented only a very small proportion of the entire school system in Shire. It was therefore decided to follow up, by questionnaire, certain key issues which had emerged from the visits and interviews. The aim of the questionnaire – undertaken in 1983 – was twofold: first, to establish whether matters mentioned regularly during interviews (such as the pupil–teacher ratio or the decreasing value of the capitation allowance) were of concern to all schools; and secondly, to establish how important these matters were to headteachers. There was a high response rate, with 79 per cent of all (276) primary schools and 88 per cent of all (52) secondary schools completing the form.

Using evidence from these sources this chapter is structured as follows. First, the broad national scene is sketched in, using mainly HMI reports together with surveys by teacher unions. A general view of the position in Shire, based upon local union surveys, is then compared with the national situation. Secondly, the position as seen from inside the schools is described using interview and questionnaire data. The main topics covered are: the physical environment; the curriculum; staffing and support; capitation.

In Chapter 3 the more nebulous, but far more worrying, problem of morale is considered.

The General Scene

HMI reports (based mainly upon first-hand observations made during visits to schools throughout the country) on the effects of local education authority expenditure policies have been published annually since 1978. They provide an ongoing assessment of the dual effects of falling rolls and expenditure cuts.

Reports by the National Union of Teachers (NUT) and the National Association of Schoolmasters and Union of Women Teachers (NAS/UWT) are based upon short questionnaires sent to a few sample schools within each area or to local representatives for completion. The data base is, therefore, far more limited than that of the HMI reports.

Furthermore, both unions are firmly opposed to the cuts, and their interpretations naturally put a different gloss on the situation compared with the more restrained neutrality of the inspectorate. And yet, despite these differences, the reports have much in common.

What emerges from all of these sources is concern for a service which is at best struggling, and at worst failing to live up to expectations and standards. This general concern is expressed in different ways, as might be expected given the different standpoints of the authors.

This dismal dossier shows the extent to which the education service is suffering from the cuts. Throughout England and Wales overworked and demoralised teachers struggle to teach children in decaying buildings. More and more parents are being asked to provide essential materials. Where parents cannot do so, their children's education suffers.

(NUT, 1982, p. 42)

Compare this with the less emotive language of the inspectorate:

At the time of their visits to institutions, HMI gained the impression of continued professional commitment and resourcefulness but of the teachers' morale worn very thin as the uncertainties and changes arising from falling rolls and cuts in expenditure affect both the maintenance of present standards and attempts to bring about improvements. For many LEA officers and teachers a particular frustration is that of being unable, because of shortages of funds and resources and tight controls on staffing, to capitalise on the benefits that could arise from the fall in pupil numbers or to respond to problems or new needs of which both officers and teachers are acutely aware.

(HMI, 1982, p. 13)

The HMI reports, over a six-year period, pick out a number of areas of continuing concern. In primary schools they note increasing numbers of larger classes, and classes containing mixed age groups; less than adequate specialist assistance within schools and advisory support from without; inadequate clerical help; too much involvement of heads in classroom teaching, thus deflecting them from their proper leadership roles; reduced provision for books and materials, and for activities such as swimming, field studies and music.

In secondary schools many similar problems were noted, but special concern was expressed for certain negative effects upon the curriculum. There is an increasing 'mismatch between the qualifications and experience of teachers and their teaching commitments'; there is 'the loss of individual subjects', including craft design and technology, modern languages, general studies, aspects of physical education and music, geology and photography; there is a fairly common 'curtailment of remedial provision and of courses for the less able including non-A-level work for children wishing to stay on after the statutory leaving age'.

The NAS/UWT report deals with all of these and provides figures indicating the number of authorities in which negative effects were reported to local secretaries. The effects seem widespread. The NUT document, concerned entirely with primary schools, provides graphic examples and accounts of particular problems experienced throughout the country. One quote (from many) will give something of the flavour of the document:

> On a recent course I was surprised how low teachers feel – not only from worry about school closure, but redeployment, salaries, resources in schools, higher pupil teacher ratios causing problems in class, vertical grouping thrust upon them by the LEA, worries about job loss and redundancy.
>
> I have never seen morale lower, but they put on brave faces and paper over the cracks – thus making it more difficult for those outside to be convinced of deterioration.
>
> (NUT, 1982, p. 40)

The general summing up of the HMI after six reports is that 'the ground is being held'. But they continue:

> Last year's report pointed out that LEAs and schools were surviving financially by doing less and that they were obliged to take less in the form it came to hand rather than by shaping it to meet educational priorities. Even with evidence of much sharper management, that is the ground that is being held. It is characterised by levels and standards of resources which are sometimes inadequate to maintain the status quo (already limited in many cases); by significant disparities between and within schools; and by schools in general being less well placed to respond constructively and enthusiastically to the many calls for educational improvement and change that come from the educational service itself and from parents and society, and which often require either extra educational range or diversification or both.
>
> (HMI, 1983, p. 10)

Embedded within this statement is an important point which is made several times in the HMI reports. It is that the status quo in some authorities is already limited, and that what is being preserved is a very low expenditure base. Shire, by its own admission, has traditionally been a relatively 'low spender' on most parts of its educational service. A report prepared by the Chief Education Officer in 1983 points out that, compared with all English non-metropolitan counties, educational expenditure in Shire generally falls in the lowest third.

This point is taken up in the NUT report on north Shire schools, and the county's 1981/2 annual report is quoted: 'Expenditure on most educational services . . . is relatively low in comparison with most Shire counties, even though its extensively rural character and higher than average proportion of smaller schools might be expected to call for greater expenditure.' This local NUT survey is based upon questionnaires returned by six comprehensive schools and twenty-four primary schools in the north of the county. The main points made in the report are as follows.

(1) Seventy per cent of the schools complained that educational provision had deteriorated as a result of staffing reductions. Some of the concerns related to reductions in the number of subjects taught, larger classes, reduced remedial teaching and practical work, mixed age group teaching and over-large reception classes.

(2) All of the schools questioned had experienced some reduction in the provision of ancillary and peripatetic help. Music teachers, welfare assistants and secretarial support were particularly mentioned.

(3) Ninety per cent expressed dissatisfaction with the state of decoration, and 50 per cent with the state of the fabric of the building.

(4) Seventy-five per cent reported a decline in teacher morale.

(5) All, bar one school, reported significant levels of parental help, particularly in fund-raising.

Another smaller (National Association of Schoolmasters and Union of Women Teachers) survey in the county, based upon responses from nine secondary and three primary schools, reported similar problems. In addition it referred to a reduction in sixth-form options, staff having to teach subjects in which they were not qualified, and increased levels of teaching for heads.

Overall the situation in Shire seems to reflect the national one, and many of the problems identified over a period by HMIs seem to apply to schools in the county. These problems are now considered in more detail.

View from the Schools

The visits made to a number of schools illustrated, amongst other things, the considerable diversity of conditions, opinions and attitudes relating to the cuts which prevailed in 1983. Whereas in one school the effects upon the curriculum, the problems of staffing, the reduction in capitation and the general state of morale were mentioned as major issues of concern, the staff in another school, not many miles away, gave quite a different view. Some teachers even suggested that, taking into account the general problems of the education service, 'they were doing not too badly'. This needs some comment.

Shire is a relatively large county and accommodates a variety of demographic features which add considerable diversity to its population. There are areas of decline but also new areas of growth. Differences can be observed not only between town and country but also between different urban and rural areas which display their own cultural, industrial and class traditions – all likely to have some effect upon attitudes towards the provision of education within the area.

There are also the 'accidents' of the past and present to consider. Take a new school built in the centre of a relatively wealthy housing development. It is purpose-built, newly decorated, fully equipped and looking forward to growth as rolls increase. The head is active and innovative and supported by a young, vigorous staff and active parent–teacher association.

Compare this situation with one in which falling rolls are having their effect; the area in general is in decline with high unemployment and increasing delinquency. The shabby school still awaits a decision concerning its future in the reorganization plan, and the head and a number of senior staff not only await, but look forward to, their retirement. Responses to questions about change will clearly be very different from both sets of staff.

There are also obvious differences between primary and secondary schools. Falling rolls have already left their mark on the primary system, leaving many schools smaller than before and many with larger than average classes. The problems associated with falling numbers are, however, just beginning to have their effect upon the secondary sector, and the questionnaire was completed before this form of contraction began to bite. Furthermore, primary and secondary schools, although similar in many respects, have their own special needs and priorities. Welfare assistance, for instance, is largely a primary school concern, whereas the range of subjects taught and the need for well-qualified specialist teachers are more likely to concern secondary heads.

An important conclusion to be drawn from the visits is that, although most schools seem to be affected by the cuts, these effects are unevenly distributed, with some schools appearing to have suffered very little and others approaching a state of what one head called 'near demoralization'. For this reason, the wider perspective provided by the questionnaire sent to all schools is important. It enables the particular problems of individual schools to be seen against the general background of opinion prevailing in the county as a whole. Using a combination of evidence obtained from visits, interviews and questionnaire responses, the various aspects of the cuts are now discussed.

(1) *The Physical Environment*
Of all matters of common concern, physical environment

was the most frequently mentioned. Most heads, except for those few in very modern schools, were keen to point out the sometimes very dilapidated state of buildings and decorations. Most were anxious to stress that deterioration did not extend to matters of safety and that the county was always swift to act where any danger was involved. Nevertheless, the dilapidation did extend beyond mere decorations, which some schools reported had not been renewed for twelve years. There were cases of leaking roofs, rotting timbers, unworkable door and window furniture and damaged boundary fences – all remaining in need of repair over a relatively long period of time.

Some schools had given up waiting for the county to carry out maintenance work and had organized teachers, caretakers and parents into working parties to undertake what were sometimes quite major redecorations. School halls, recently painted in this way, were pointed out by heads with a mixture of pride and exasperation.

In some schools it was reported either that furniture and fittings had not been supplied in the first place (one school head reported buying some equipment second-hand) or that damaged items had remained unrepaired and unusable for months and even years.

Some schools reported that it was becoming more difficult to obtain the regular maintenance of playing-fields, and there were complaints of pitches having to be abandoned for periods of time awaiting grass cutting.

The extent of shared discomfort as the physical environment worsens is apparent from the questionnaire returns. Out of 214 primary school responses, 142 noted a decrease in the maintenance of buildings since 1978, and of these 81 complained of a major decrease. Thirty-one of the 44 responses to this question by secondary school heads noted a decrease in maintenance, and 19 of these referred to a major decrease.

In order to ascertain the degree of concern that heads attached to the various effects of the cuts, they were asked to select five items from a list of fourteen and rank them in order of importance. The maintenance of buildings regularly appeared in the first five choices and in all was mentioned 122 times. On this basis it stands as the sixth most important item of concern within the list of fourteen items.

The conclusion to be drawn from this is that most schools have suffered to some extent from lack of maintenance. Heads regard the problem as important but not of the highest priority. As was pointed out many times, however, the apparent savings made in this area may prove to be false in the longer term as the costs of making good accumulate.

(2) *The Curriculum*

The HMI and NUT reports mentioned earlier indicate not only a concern to protect, expand and update the curriculum but also an acknowledgement that these aims are being thwarted by the cuts. The local NUT report also indicates some erosion of provision within Shire. Heads and teachers at most of the secondary schools visited expressed their concern that certain subjects had had to be dropped from the curriculum or taught to fewer pupils.

Spanish was one subject removed from the curriculum in one secondary school visited. In another, modern language is taught only to the top of the ability range after the first year. The same school has reduced its fourth- and fifth-year options by about one-fifth. Another comprehensive school has severely cut the number of O- and A-level options, and has lost geology, engineering drawing, woodcraft and needlecraft. There can be little doubt that some schools are feeling the effects of the cuts on parts of the curriculum.

It might, therefore, be expected that the problem would show up in the questionnaire responses and indicate a general level of concern. In fact few schools reported a decrease in the number of subjects taught. Overall, out of 254 schools responding to the questionnaire, 143 replied 'little change', only 32 mentioned a decrease, and 79 reported an increase. For primary schools only, out of 203 responses, 22 reported a decrease, and 126 noted little change. In the secondary group, out of 45, only 9 reported a decrease, whereas 20 reported an increase.

Furthermore, concern over reductions in the number of subjects taught was relatively low as a problem in the order of priorities. It came only twelfth out of fourteen. This clearly needs some explanation, for it appears to contrast with other findings discussed earlier.

Although some subjects are being lost or restricted there is still a certain amount of curriculum innovation taking place. In the primary schools the introduction of the micro-computer has led to curriculum changes in many schools and may account for the number of responses indicating an increase in the number of subjects taught.

In the secondary schools various changes have also been taking place. Computer studies now regularly appear on the timetable, and there is also an increase in business or vo-cationally oriented subjects. There is already some evidence that the Technical and Vocational Education Initiative (TVEI) and the influence of the Business and Technical Education Council (BTEC) are having their effect, particularly upon the curriculum at the top end of a number of schools.

Some schools also report an increase in the number of CSE subjects introduced to offer scope to children at the lower end of the ability range. The unemployment situation has also resulted in greater numbers of children staying on into the sixth form, and this has caused some schools to add new subjects to cope with this new demand.

Overall, it seems that the effect of recession upon the curriculum has been mixed, with some schools suffering more than others. But also, offsetting the decline in some traditional areas of the curriculum, there has been a growth in other, newer subject areas.

One further point should be mentioned before leaving the curriculum issue. Several schools reported an increase in the number of children needing special help. Many pupils in this group were unable to cope with traditionally taught subjects at levels expected for their age. It is in this area of special teaching that curriculum developments may be needed (and this will become more important as the provisions of the

1981 Education Act are implemented in schools). But it is also in this area that pressures on staffing are being increasingly felt.

(3) *Staffing and Support*

In this section the teaching process itself and the support needed for teachers to function effectively are considered. First, are there enough teachers to do the job? The simple answer upon which most officers, councillors and teachers would agree is, No, not in an ideal world. But in the context of education in recession the feeling is that the position at present is reasonable.

This is due in part to the county's curriculum/staffing policy, usually referred to as its curriculum model. Sometimes called curriculum-led staffing, the model calculates the number of teachers needed in a school according to the number of classes formed, the subjects taught, the length of time devoted to each and the appropriate group size. The model, which is discussed in more detail in a later chapter (see page 114), has helped to provide a cushion against falling rolls and has commanded widespread support across the county. It represents for many a bulwark protecting traditional pupil–teacher ratios.

For some, these ratios still leave room for improvement, but at least the position, as represented by the model, is (or was until 1981) no worse than before and for some it is slightly better. What was resented, though, by many of the heads interviewed was the 1981 cut in staffing (of a hundred teachers), which was the first real taste of staffing pressure that many schools had felt. The following statements indicate the depth of feeling:

> The cut in the curriculum model is largely to blame for many of my current difficulties.

> The cut has meant the loss of a full post to me.

But not all schools were affected in this way, and some heads had no complaints – so far. 'It's a matter of juggling with figures,' said one, 'but it usually works out all right in the end.'

The questionnaire responses indicate two things. First, they show that the pupil–teacher ratio is near the top of the list of priorities for heads in both primary and secondary sectors. It comes a close second to the problem of staff morale. Secondly, the responses indicate that since 1978 the ratios have held steady. In the secondary schools 9 reported a decrease, 17 an increase, and 22 little change. In the primary sector 76 reported an increase, 117 little change, and 68 a decrease. Thus, as regards numbers of teachers, although the matter is of considerable concern to heads, and many have fears for the future, the position in 1983 was regarded as relatively satisfactory.

On another aspect of staffing, most of the schools visited complained about the effect of the cuts upon their ability to employ ancillary and part-time staff of one kind or another. There were marked differences between primary and secondary schools in this respect. In the primary schools the main problem referred to was the loss of welfare assistants and reductions in the availability of part-time and peripatetic teachers, particularly those concerned with remedial work, science and music.

Questionnaire responses indicated the extent of this problem. In respect of part-time and specialist teachers, over half of the schools reported a decrease since 1978, and of these more than half complained of a major decrease. With regard to welfare assistance, the picture is clear: 100 schools reported a major decrease, and a further 20 a small decrease.

Another area in which primary schools appear to have felt the pressure is the availability of clerical assistance, where 53 reported a major decrease, and 59 a minor one. It should also be noted that the questionnaire returns confirm the interview data that these support facilities are important to schools. Welfare assistance ranks fourth, and clerical assistance fifth, in order of importance.

In the secondary schools there was less concern over the question of ancillary staff either in interviews or from the questionnaire data. Clerical assistance was, however, mentioned many times, and the questionnaire responses indicate that about one-third of the schools have been affected. Heads also put it fifth on their list of priorities.

(4) *Capitation*

An important aspect of teaching and curriculum development is the equipment and materials available for use in the classrooms and school libraries. These are built up and maintained largely through the capitation allowance per pupil each year. Considerable importance is attached to the annual figures by the educational press, unions and other pressure groups, and annual league tables are published showing comparisons between authorities. Shire has tended, over the years, to be in the lower half of the table. Heads place the matter high on their list of priorities. For all schools it ranks fourth. Secondary heads placed it third.

The topic was mentioned by heads during most visits but with some variation in opinion. Some schools felt that the allowance had not kept pace with inflation and had left their resources depleted over the years. Others were reasonably happy with the amounts received although always admitting that they could use more.

Generally it was primary schools, where the allowance is lower, where the cuts seemed to be felt far more, and this is reflected in the questionnaire responses. Out of 260 replies, 154 reported a decrease in the value of the capitation allowance over the five years prior to 1983, and of these 62 had noted a major decrease. In secondary schools, however, the responses were fairly balanced, with as many heads pointing to an increase as to a decrease.

This may be partly accounted for by the size of the school. A small school will obviously receive a smaller sum than a large school and therefore will have less flexibility in spending. The larger school with more to spend, in effect, reaps certain economies of scale if the materials are carefully spread, maintained and re-used.

The overall position with regard to physical resources, staffing and the curriculum can be summed up as one of concern but, in the majority of cases, of just about coping. Clear exceptions exist at either end of the scale. The maintenance of buildings is an area of growing concern, and it is felt that the longer the position is allowed to deteriorate the more the problem will accumulate.

There are, however, other, possibly more serious consequences of the cuts, and these are considered next.

3

The Schools: Social Climate and Response to Adversity

In Chapter 2 the main focus of interest was the physical deprivations of the schools, staffing shortages and the effects of the cuts on the curriculum. In this chapter we turn to matters of morale and to the responses which some parents and schools are making to overcome the effects of the recession.

There seems little doubt, in the opinion of those interviewed and responding to the Shire questionnaire, that the social climate in schools has changed over the past five years. These changes, admittedly due to a combination of factors including the cuts, have had a negative effect on morale – a key ingredient of the social climate. It is worth looking first at the responses of 263 headteachers to the question regarding the morale of staff.

One hundred and sixty-five reported a decrease in morale, and of these 57 noted a major decrease. There was little difference between primary and secondary schools in their replies to this question. Heads in both sectors also placed this issue as their top priority. Furthermore, in secondary schools, heads reported a decline in the morale of pupils in about a third of the schools, and all heads in this sector put pupil morale fourth in order of importance in their list of concerns.

These responses were all made before the difficulties and antagonisms engendered by the 1985 round of negotiations on pay and conditions of service. It will be recalled that the National Union of Teachers withdrew from these as a protest against what was seen as an attempt by the government to impose unacceptable conditions of service upon the profession – including an appraisal scheme for teachers which might be linked, in some way, to pay and promotion. This action paved the way to the often turbulent events of the 1985 school year.

But what is morale, and how are changes manifested in the social climate of the schools? These questions are considered using observations made on visits in 1983/4 coupled with interview data. One (old) dictionary seems to capture the essence of morale as it applies to the current situation: 'mental state, especially as regards zeal, determination, hope, devotion, and the like which may make a man or body of men capable of endurance and of persevering with courage in the presence of danger, fatigue, discouragement, etc.' (*The Simplified Dictionary*, Virtue & Co.).

It is this mental state of the individual and the group which has undergone change in the past few years. Zeal, determination, hope and devotion have been reduced in the presence of fatigue and discouragement (and possibly even danger in the form of potential job loss). The reasons for the decline and their implications for schools are complex. Some indication of the seriousness of the situation and the factors which underlie individual mental states can be derived from statements made by senior teachers, of which the following is fairly typical.

> I now work much longer hours than in the past. If you worked statutory hours you wouldn't get the job done. But the satisfaction has gone. You feel beleaguered and under siege with carping from the press, complaints from parents and always calls for more accountability and further savings. All this stultifies initiative.
>
> Teachers generally are putting in far more hours and they are feeling the pressures without the rewards. Many of them are simply looking towards early retirement to get out of it as soon as they can.

It is clear, however, that these attitudes are not solely and directly the result of the cuts. There is a feeling amongst many teachers that the whole system is under closer scrutiny than ever before, both nationally and locally, and that

autonomy, and with it the feeling of competent professionalism, is being eroded. One head described himself as a
'glorified form-filler', and officers admit that the amount of
information and statistics required from schools has
increased considerably in recent years. In addition there is
considerable change to be accommodated in both the curriculum and the assessment system. Many complained of the
fact that this was often imposed with little or no consultation
and increased the sense of uncertainty.

If morale is, at least partly, to do with leadership, then
some heads certainly feel that traditional ways and means of
leading have gradually been eroded. The excitement of the
possibility of bringing about social change and economic
betterment through education has largely gone. In the secondary schools in particular the looming prospect of
unemployment for school-leavers filters back even into the
lower forms.

The teachers themselves feel trapped with little hope of
promotion within the school or county system and even less
hope of an upward move to another area. The mental state of
depression is reinforced by an everyday reality reflected in
decaying buildings, damaged furniture and shortages of
equipment and materials. This is made worse by the fact that
the cuts, originally regarded as a short-term measure, seem
destined to continue and in secondary schools to be accompanied by further cut-backs and anxieties associated with
falling rolls.

There is also another aspect of the social climate which,
although controversial, is for many heads and teachers an
important, but fast disappearing, feature of school life. This
is the school meals provision. In most schools the service has
been completely reorganized with a number of food sources
now available. Some children avail themselves of school
dinners, others bring packed lunches; some buy food from
the snack bar, and others from mobile shops which park
adjacent to the school or from the local fish-and-chip shop.
There are many teachers who regret that the social cohesion
that they felt was engendered by 'all sitting down together'
has been lost.

The picture, then, is not a happy one and it bears a close resemblance to the general observations made by the HMI (1981) report: 'Nevertheless there is evidence that teachers' morale has been adversely affected in many schools. Its weakening, if it became widespread, would pose a major problem in the effort to maintain standards, let alone improve them.' But depression and gloom are not universal, and there have been responses to the situation which are important. Whether they are of the kind that teachers, officers and parents think should occur is a matter of debate and concern.

Challenge and Response

There are a number of schools where the cuts do not seem to have had any adverse effect. There are, for instance, a few in areas where rolls have not decreased and they have grown or remained stable in numbers. By comparison with their less fortunate neighbours they appear to the outsider, and often to staff within them, to have fared relatively well. It is not these schools that are of interest here, but rather those that have had to cope with cuts and have sought other ways of maintaining or improving their position.

Taking first place in the 'self-help league' is the support – financial and otherwise – of parents. This factor is outstandingly demonstrated in the questionnaire returns. It is clearly shown in Table 3.1.

Table 3.1 *Change in financial help from parents since 1978*

	Primary	*Secondary*
Major decrease	9	—
Minor decrease	14	4
Little change	52	18
Minor increase	54	11
Major increase	86	12

In effect nearly two-thirds of all schools responding had noted an increase in parental contributions. Half of these, or about one-third of the schools in Shire, reported a major increase. This accords with the HMI 1983 report which states that 'at the school level, over two-thirds of all returns made by HMI on their visits judged parental contributions to be moderate or substantial' (p. 13).

But what does 'substantial' mean in real terms? This became clear during the visits. The ways of raising money were varied and creative. Generally, but not always, parent–teacher associations (PTAs) were the main driving force. They are relied upon by many schools to raise anything from £500 to several thousand pounds annually. Covenants were also mentioned on a few occasions where parents or PTAs guarantee an annual amount, such as £10 or more per child.

One head commented that when the PTA was set up originally it was agreed that it should not be a fund-raising body, but 'Now I rely upon them desperately.' This PTA has equipped the school orchestra and provided a minibus for travel.

The use to which money is put, however, is very varied. One PTA had set itself a target of £5,000 to help re-stock the school library. Another had raised money on a matched funding basis with the authority, and parents had themselves built an extension to the main building. Another had bought and erected a terrapin building. Almost all schools reported help from parents with decorating and minor repairs.

Parents were also to be found helping within the school. This was not only the traditional 'listening to them read' but helping prepare learning materials, stock-taking, clerical help and providing transport for visits.

Parents and PTAs, however, were not the only source of help. In some schools, heads had taken it upon themselves to create a miniature and partially self-supporting enterprise. The story of one school, although unique because of the scale of its response, contains ideas and activities which some other schools have adopted. The school concerned is a primary school which, because it has become well known in its locality, now attracts children from a distance and no longer suffers the effects of falling rolls. Pupils carry out certain administrative tasks, and the visitor is likely to be met and looked after by a junior pupil until the head, who does his share of teaching, is found. Coffee is made and served to visitors by the children. The school has an atmosphere of liveliness, and the curriculum whilst still maintaining basic subjects is largely project-based and uses field trips at home and abroad as a stimulus to learning. The Hebrides and Greece are two areas visited in recent years.

The head's response in answer to a question about the cuts was: 'My attitude is to ignore them; the children only have one chance, so let's make the best of it.'

There is plenty of help from parents, and the PTA has guaranteed £10 a year per child. But that is not enough to cover the trips; money has to be raised elsewhere. 'Industry is always prepared to help if approached in the right way' – the head had spent three days in the Midlands the previous week and raised enough money to cover the still outstanding costs for the Greek trip. Both the BBC and the local government in Greece were interested in the journey.

The head had also managed to persuade a well-known computer firm to install free of charge several micro-computers in the school as an experiment.

The staff were enthusiastic and, it seemed, worked very much longer hours than normal but with the prospect of at least some job satisfaction at the end. There was criticism of the situation which forced schools to act in this way but, given prevailing conditions, this is how it had to be, and they would get on with it.

This profile is included to illustrate the point that schools are surviving and some even thriving in difficult circumstances. But the matter is regarded by many as unsatisfactory. Parental support is clearly taking on an ever increasing role in 'covering the cracks' as one teacher put it. The question must be asked, How are the 40 per cent of schools that have not received increased financial support from parents faring? The point is made in nearly all the HMI reports that parental contributions create their own problems. The following from the 1982 and 1983 reports sound the warning:

> Schools are turning increasingly to parents and the local community for financial help. Some schools have a long tradition of raising funds to pay for educational visits and desirable but expensive items of equipment. Funds are now frequently used to provide basic materials and equipment. This trend is leading to marked disparities of provision between schools serving affluent and poor areas.
>
> (1982, p. 13)

> Parental contributions to the costs of education were widespread. Beneficial as these are to the schools concerned, they have become an important factor in widening the differences in resources available to schools.
>
> (1983, p. 13)

In summary, then, it seems that schools in Shire have been considerably affected by the recession both physically and in terms of morale.

Decisions were explicitly made by the local education authority to protect, as far as possible, pupil–teacher ratios, and this inevitably resulted in cuts elsewhere; mainly in the supporting fabric of the system. Looked at in the context of total educational expenditure in Shire the cuts have not been large but they have been sufficient to cause shortages and delays involving many aspects of the school system which had hitherto been regarded as important, if not essential. Partly because of this, but for other reasons also (not least, more recently, the negotiations on pay and conditions of service), morale has suffered, and the general social climate of schools has declined as a result. In some respects this might be regarded as the most important negative outcome.

There were other policy options which might have been, but were not, considered in Shire. Whether they would have resulted in better or worse outcomes is impossible to say. The only conclusion that can be drawn with any certainty is that changes have occurred as a result of policy decisions and these have caused problems for many schools. The problems are of both a physical and psychological nature, and it is the combination of these two conditions which creates the sense of frustration and injustice felt in many schools.

Part II examines the conditions and policies which have led up to this situation and the way in which Shire and most other local authorities have dealt with the problem of recession. The story is at times complicated and involved and depends upon politics and personalities as well as organizational and budgetary factors. These are all considered in the following chapters.

PART II

Cultures of Choice

During the early stages of the project, when councillors were being interviewed about their part in policy-making, one senior Labour member who had spent many years in local government remarked that some officers in Shire Hall actually seemed to enjoy making cuts. He felt that it exercised them in quite a creative way, and that expertise in seeking out and suggesting ways in which savings might be made could even lead to promotion.

Further elaboration of this point led to the mention of a 'cuts culture'. This brought an immediate positive response from the councillor and resulted in a discussion as to how the style of policy-making and the whole feel of the organization had changed over a decade.

Although senior officers, with whom the idea was later discussed, disagreed with the possibility that some people enjoyed making cuts, or that promotion might be had from it, they did respond to the notion of a cuts culture. They were interested to compare the differences between a cuts culture and a growth culture. The idea was gradually developed and refined over the course of the study and eventually provided the structure for the main part of this book.

'Culture' is used in this context to denote the general state or condition of an organization brought about by a set of factors, the most important of which are values, customs and beliefs about the way things should be done. The term is usually associated with society as a whole, but subcultures have long been recognized, and the concept is transferable to other contexts. Handy (1976), for instance, talks of organizational cultures in the following way:

> In organisations there are deep seated beliefs about the way work should be organised, the way authority should be exercised, people rewarded, people controlled. What are the degrees of formalisation required? How much planning and how far ahead? . . . Do committees control or individuals? Are there rules and procedures or only results? These are all parts of the culture of an organisation.
>
> (p. 177)

It is these conditions, which prevail within an organization, which create the cultures of choice. Often the culture of an organization reflects the prevailing culture of the society in which it exists. Thus a growth culture within an organization may be part of an overall condition of growth within the economy. But this is not always the case, and there will be times when certain industries or sectors of the economy are growing whilst other parts are contracting. The cultures within local government have tended to follow the national economic climate but, as will be seen, not entirely so and not always at the same time.

Why 'cultures of *choice*'? The argument followed here is that policy-making takes place within a set of cultural conditions, and these conditions have an important influence on choice. The cultural mode may sometimes open up choice and lead to the wider scanning of alternatives or it may restrict choice and leave available only limited courses of action. Thus in a cuts culture there may be no option other than to reduce the budget – but there are usually several ways in which this can be done. The choice then is not whether to cut but where to cut.

This study indicates that these conditions of choice have changed radically over three decades. It is suggested that four distinct cultures can be identified which considerably affect the organization and its policy-making style and procedures. Since 1944 Shire and many other authorities have experienced this sequence of cultures brought about mainly by changes in the resources available and the conditions under which they have been made available.

These changes have, in turn, resulted in two major effects:

(1)   a shift from a state of growth to one of contraction; and
(2)   a vacillation between conditions of relative certainty to those of uncertainty.

In some respects the two factors may seem to be linked in so far as greater certainty is usually associated with growth, and uncertainty with contraction. But this need not be so, and it is possible for rapid growth to be accompanied by uncertainty leading to *ad hoc* unplanned decisions, and for contraction to be deliberately controlled through the use of various budgetary or administrative devices.

The two factors can, in fact, be viewed as quite separate elements or dimensions. One dimension extends from growth to contractions; the other extends from extreme uncertainty to reasonable certainty. If these two dimensions are plotted diagrammatically as intersecting axes they form a matrix from which four cultures can be derived – see Figure II.1.

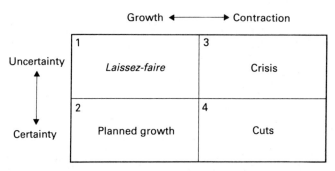

Figure II.1   *Cultures of choice*

From the figure it is clear that the main underlying conditions of the four cultures are:

(1) *'laissez-faire'* – growth accompanied by uncertainty;
(2) 'planned growth' – expansion with (at least, relative) certainty;
(3) 'crisis' – contraction with uncertainty (often extreme); and, finally,
(4) 'cuts' – contraction associated with greater certainty.

Parts II and III of the book analyse these cultures and follow education in Shire through their progression. The exact transition from one to another is not always clear. There may be overlap or the coexistence of features from more than one culture at the same time but, generally, it is possible to identify a dominance of one culture over the others.

In Chapter 4 the *laissez-faire* culture is seen emerging after the early lean postwar years and gaining impetus into the 1960s. It is a period when attitudes and expectations towards growth and the place of education in an expanding economy were being formed and set. Chapter 5 describes how *laissez-faire* was challenged by the idea of rational planning, and how attempts were made to bring *ad hoc* spending under control and provide new guidelines for expenditure based upon carefully assessed priorities.

Crisis followed planned growth as the economy faltered and severe limits were placed on local government spending by central government. This is the age of contraction and is dealt with in Chapters 6 and 7, which cover respectively: the meaning and effects of crisis in local government; and educational policy-making in Shire in a time of contraction.

The discussion of an emerging cuts culture begins Part III. Within such a culture there are many important but uncomfortable issues for professional service departments, especially education, to consider. What is more, the cuts culture may become an enduring feature of organizational life. The implications of this, especially for education, are considered in the concluding chapters.

4

Laissez-faire

Laissez-faire literally means 'let alone', 'let people do as they please'. In economics it is used to denote non-interference by government in business affairs. Here it is used to indicate a relative freedom in the educational system to take action and to spend money according to immediately perceived local needs. This does not mean that there was no central policy on education, nor that local authorities or other agencies were completely autonomous in their decision-making – but rather that, compared with later periods when planning and central control took on far greater significance, there was a period of rapid growth accompanied by a relative freedom of action.

In terms of the economy in general, the immediate post-war years heralded a period of national reconstruction. They provided expansion and growth but from a very low base. They were accompanied by shortages, rationing and bottle-necks. It was a time of austerity and consumer shortages which were necessary to facilitate investment and growth.

But by 1950 the scene and the mood were beginning to change, and policy-making was, to a large extent, based on the assumption of annual economic growth. Medium- and long-term plans for the economy were linked to forecasts of a 4 or 5 per cent increase in gross national product every year. It was confidently expected that increased consumer spending, matched by increased export sales, would lead to greater investment, which in turn would create more jobs and lead to still higher spending. This 'multiplier effect' was accepted and revered by governments of all political persuasions.

Industrial and commercial organizations were automatically expected to increase in size, and this expectation was extended to local government as well. A classic economic text of the time was *The Theory of the Growth of the Firm* (Penrose, 1959). It was natural for organisms to grow – why not the firm and the economy also? The naturalness of decline was seldom discussed; it was a taboo subject like serious illness and death.

The cultural mood of the age eventually became one of 'never had it so good' optimism, and in this frame of mind new ideas and experiments flourished. It was, in a way, a 'youth culture'. There was much to look forward to, risks could be taken, new personal and social encounters and relationships tried. The term 'permissive society' was much used. It seemed to imply permission to try new things without the threat of sanctions. The culture generally became more extrovert and open in its ideas, art forms and approaches to education.

Education and *Laissez-faire*

The postwar Labour government had a difficult task. As Kogan (1975) points out:

> Amidst steel and timber rationing, a recurrent shortage of labour, a serious imbalance between pupil numbers and trained teachers, it did its best to implement the 1944 Act by providing secondary education for all up to the age of fifteen, by ensuring that there were at least roofs over the children's heads, by remanning the schools through the emergency teacher training system, and by the first build-up of further education.
>
> (p. 27)

The long consumer boom began after the Suez Crisis in 1956, and the attitudinal and social changes associated with this era were reflected in the expansion of education, where at one time it was claimed that schools were being built at the rate of one per day.

Figures produced by Vaizey and Sheehan (1968) indicate

the extent of the financial growth of expenditure on education. They show, for instance, that between 1950 and 1965 expenditure (at constant prices) on primary education had grown from £78 to £100 million, on secondary education from £57 to £118 million and on further education from £15 to £45 million (p. 156). These figures, it should be noted, are after allowing for the effects of inflation.

Furthermore, as the National Income and Expenditure Survey for 1973 shows, expenditure on education as a proportion of national income rose from 3.38 per cent in 1951 to 5.53 per cent in 1965, and the trend continued, reaching 7.35 per cent by 1973.

A report by the Society of Education Officers (SEO, 1974) referred to the sense of achievement felt in the education service at the beginning of the 1970s:

> In 1970 there was some joy in the education service in the UK because total spending on the service in that year overtook spending on defence . . . Between 1959 and 1970 the average annual increase in expenditure on education was consistently higher than other public expenditure, higher than increases in GNP and higher than increases in consumer expenditure. For example in the decade 1960–70, 51% more was spent on education in real terms: yet only 10% more on food; 35% more on radio, television and so on; 44% more on alcohol (but 70% more on cars).
>
> (p. 61)

What lay behind this rapid and sustained growth? There were probably three main factors. The first impetus to growth was the opposite to that which is so important in the 1980s – increasing rather than falling rolls. The postwar years had seen a rapid rise in the birth rate, and by the early 1950s the education service was having to cater for a steadily increasing school population. As time went on not only did more children enter the schools, but a growing number decided to stay on beyond the statutory leaving age. In 1950 there were 5.9 million children in maintained and assisted schools and in 1970 there were 8.4 million – an increase of just over 40 per cent (DES, 1973).

Expenditure in real terms had increased by more than this. Also, given that the larger schools then being built would normally result in falling unit costs, it seems that education was receiving more money than could be accounted for purely on the basis of an increase in pupil numbers.

The second reason for the education boom was an economic and social one. Education was regarded as having an answer to many of the problems that industrialized countries were facing in the postwar era. Vaizey (1962), addressing the issue 'education for tomorrow', makes the case strongly for a new and improved education service to meet the needs of a rapidly changing and highly competitive world. He argues that many of the economic and social problems – including poor performance in world markets, failure to create maximum growth in the economy, lack of a skilled technical workforce, the acceptance of amateurism in industry and commerce, the squalid state of UK cities compared with those of other European countries, and the increasing level of delinquency – could all, in part at least, be traced to an inadequate and inappropriate education system: 'It is the seriousness of this social and intellectual crisis which makes the rapid re-adaption of our educational system an essential basis for a developing economy' (p. 24).

The 'economics of education' was also taking root as a respectable academic subject, and early theories were pointing to a correlation between expenditure on education and economic growth. Whether this was a cause-and-effect relationship, and in which direction, was not clear, but the message that there might be an important link was one that appeared to influence policy-makers. The extent of the work done in this field at that time is well documented by Blaug (1970).

The third reason for the expansion was, no doubt, linked to the second but it was manifest in an extraordinary interest in education by the general public and a level of popularity which contrasts starkly with the tarnished image which education carries in the 1980s. This phenomenon of the mid-1960s is considered by Regan (1977):

One of the most interesting aspects of contemporary British culture is the enormous favour accorded education by all sections of the populace. Expenditure on other services either receives less positive support (health, social services) or is decidedly contentious (roads, defence, nationalised industries). In the term used by Sir Bruce Fraser, former Comptroller and Auditor General, education has top 'political sex appeal'.

(p. 193)

Both Vaizey and Sheehan (1968) and Kogan (1975) regard the period between 1955 and 1965, during which Sir David Eccles completed two terms as Minister of Education, as one of the most important in the expansionist era. But as Kogan points out it was a period rolling forward on a tide of uncertainty.

Eccles rode on this tide. He wanted to improve rather than to radically change the system. He found that expansion was favoured in general terms but that no one was clear about how to use the money . . .
Eccles worked comfortably within the 1944 Act, which was both expansionist and non-partisan. To him, teaching standards were more important than structure and he sponsored the boom in teacher supply and the large building programme.

(p. 33)

The key point made above is that no one was very clear about how to use the money. It was a time to grow, to innovate and to experiment. For the educational policy-maker it was a time for raising and spending money. Estimates and budgets that did not build in development and improvement funding were more likely to be questioned than those that did. If local funds could not be raised there was always the possibility of central government support or grants from one of the many funding agencies with a special interest in education. Money seemed readily available to stimulate and support change.

Levine (1978), commenting on policy-making in general, suggests that: 'Under conditions of abundance, habit, snap judgements and other forms of informal analysis will suffice for most decisions because the costs of making mistakes can easily be absorbed without threatening the organisation's survival' (p. 317).

Policy-making within this culture also bore a close relationship to what Braybrooke and Lindblom (1970) call 'disjointed incrementalism'. In this there is a series of relatively small changes (which may, overall, account for a large change) brought about in conditions of low understanding concerning their outcomes. They maintain:

> It is decision making through small or incremental moves on particular problems rather than through a comprehensive reform program. It is also endless: it takes the form of an indefinite sequence of policy moves. Moreover it is exploratory in that the goals of policy making continue to change as new experience with policy throws new light on what is possible and desirable. In this sense, it is also better described as moving away from the known social ills rather than as moving toward a known and relatively stable goal.
>
> (p. 71)

Furthermore, it is a disjointed process in that many agencies are likely to be chipping away at the same problem quite independently of each other, or as Braybrooke and Lindblom suggest: 'Analysis of any single given problem area and of possible policies for solving the problem is often conducted in a large number of centers.'

There are other decision process theories which portray a similar picture. In these, organizations are viewed as contexts in which people and problems are mixed and solutions emerge. Outcomes are determined by the process itself and by the constraints on that process, and they are not predictable (March and Olsen, 1976; Mackenzie, 1978).

This is largely true of policy-making in the *laissez-faire* culture. Serious questioning of goals, careful consideration of alternative courses of action, monitoring or evaluation of the changes, if and when they occur, are carried out in a rather perfunctory way or are not given great prominence. The cultural norm is: 'let's try it and quickly'.

Turbulence in the system was considerable as ideas proliferated and traditional views were challenged. Radical views were treated with some interest. Writing in the late 1960s under the general theme of radical school reform were, amongst others, Goodman (1971), Holt (1971), Illich (1971), Postman and Weingartner (1971), Reimer (1971) and Freire (1972). Their criticism centred upon the oppressive, deliberalizing, uniform, compulsory nature of education and the control which schools exercised over what should be learned and how it should be learned. It created, in Freire's terms, 'domesticated' students.

A progressive movement was beginning in primary schools. Underpinning it were ideas relating to a child's ability to learn more effectively in conditions which allowed greater freedom. Hence there was more concern for the individual child, for exploratory, heuristic, or discovery learning and for more open environments in which pupils could move more freely, less restricted by time, space and teacher direction.

In the secondary schools the aims of schooling and the curriculum itself were in a state of flux. Taylor (1971), discussing the shortcomings of the system, illustrates the uncertainties of the situation facing educationists:

> Alas, the imperatives are now simply too many and too various, defying inclusion and coherence. Secondary education has become a bazaar of rival propositions: every adult from his memory, every parent from his heart, every taxpayer from his pocket, every employer from his need, reckons he has the right to speak his mind. Now boys themselves have suggestions to offer, and people will seek their opinions. The Schools Council recently conducted a survey among present and former schoolboys, and teachers and parents, on the importance of various aims of secondary education. The answers revealed a complete, a comic disarray.
>
> (p. 141)

On the subject of curriculum reform he continues:

> The growing fear that the learner might die of excess has been a major impetus behind recent curriculum reform. New courses have been devised which superannuate a lot of the time-consuming, traditional material, and rearrange the remainder in a more logical economic order (though mysteriously what is finally included seems always to take up more time than ever). The touchstone of what to discard and what to retain or introduce is 'relevance', a much-used term in current curricular argument and one which, like the older notion of 'useful', conceals radical divergence.
>
> (p. 20)

To help sort out the possibilities came, amongst others, the Schools Council, the National Foundation for Educational Research, the Nuffield Foundation and the Council for Educational Technology, all supporting projects and developments which hoped to throw some light upon educational change and offer guidance to teacher and decision-maker alike. Ultimately they presented an exciting and varied but utterly confusing range of possibilities.

The scene was changing very fast indeed, and it was at this time that the teachers' innovation joke was generally heard: 'Don't worry if you miss this educational bandwagon, there's another one right behind!' Bandwagons do, however, lose momentum and eventually they did stop coming, or at least operated on a much reduced service on routes planned in much greater detail and with both political and resource considerations in mind.

The relatively non-partisan approach towards education referred to by Kogan above, aimed at the fulfilment of the intentions of the 1944 Act, continued in a more or less *laissez-faire* fashion until Labour came into office in 1964. Even then expansion continued, particularly at the secondary and higher education levels, but behind the expansion lay policies based upon the redistribution of social opportunities. These policies not only led to a rapid growth in the number of universities and the advent of the polytechnics, but also to the important Circular 10/65 on comprehensive education and proposals for educational priority areas and urban aid.

Laissez-faire was by the late 1960s beginning to give way to a period of policy-directed growth eventually merging into a planned growth culture as described in the next chapter. There is no precise date for the change, and the *laissez-faire* period contained elements of planned growth just as the planned growth period contained a degree of *laissez-faire*; but for those who experienced both periods, the differences were striking.

Laissez-faire in Shire

What was Shire like during this period of rapid and sustained growth through the 1950s and most of the 1960s? What made it a *laissez-faire* culture and what was it like to participate in policy-making in those days?

The present County Treasurer, looking back to this period, found it 'the most uncomfortable of my career – there was no sense of priority nor direction'. This is indicative of the relative degree of autonomy which existed for local government and for the separate services within it – which, from the standpoint of the treasurer, appeared to be operating in a *laissez-faire* fashion. To appreciate why this was so and what the implications were, some explanation of the policy-making process in Shire, which had much in common with many other shire counties, is necessary.

The County Club
Most of the business was conducted in the main 'Shire Hall', a building relatively new but just old enough to have lifts enclosed in wire cages with metal trellis-type gates. It was, and still is, essentially in two parts: a councillor (and in those days, alderman) area, and the officers' rooms mainly on the floors above. The former is plush, almost regal, with an imposing staircase bedecked with oil-paintings; off the high,

wide corridor there are imposing and expensively furnished meeting rooms. The feeling is one of tasteful affluence.

In contrast the officers' rooms are functional and set in rows off anonymous corridors and staircases. Their size and the quality of furniture and fittings, however, vary with status in the hierarchy. The separation of the councillors and officers is more than just physical, for, except for special points of contact (e.g. the regular meetings of a chief officer and the chairman of his departmental committee), they represent two distinct worlds.

The councillors' world, in the days of *laissez-faire*, was described by various members as 'most civilized' or 'like a club'. It was a place 'you looked forward to going to and exchanging news with old friends and colleagues'. This is in stark contrast with the contemporary world of crisis and cuts, and there are clear reasons for this.

First and foremost was the fact that growth seemed assured, and finance was readily available to meet almost whatever needs were identified. It was more a matter of keeping up with available funds than finding the money for projects. This situation avoided the need to compete with colleagues over the allocation of funds. As the Chief Executive, then treasurer, put it: 'the underlying assumption behind policy was one of growth and improvement and not simply maintaining services'.

But there were other reasons related to an overall consensus on major issues; a strong feeling of local autonomy and an acceptance of the right and duty of each member to look after the interests of his or her own constituency. These factors require some elaboration.

Local Autonomy

Shire Council in those days was dominated by Conservatives, although about one-third of the elected members stood as non-political or Independent. Many council members regarded themselves as 'apolitical'. A senior Conservative office-holder made it clear that he considered himself to be 'part of local government but not in local politics'. Furthermore, the prevailing attitude amongst the members was one of primary loyalties to Shire and to their consti-tuency within it. If there was conflict between these, mem-bers could expect a reasonable and fair hearing from their colleagues as they put their case. A compromise could usually be reached.

Generally, there were meetings of the party group before all major committees but these seldom lasted more than an hour. They were fairly informal, and there was no strong leadership. In fact leadership in the Conservative group has, in the past, been an uncertain affair and has tended to be shared between three roles: Chairman of Council, Deputy Chairman of Council and Party Chairman. Dominance has often shifted with changes in personality.

Councillors were, for the most part, not Conservatives in the national sense, nor did they expect interference from central government. There was sufficient consensus of values to provide adequate policy guidelines on most matters without instructions from central office.

Gyford and James (1982), considering party political linkages between centre and periphery, point out:

> It could also be the case that the local and national elements of the party for the most part go their own ways. Thus Bulpitt has suggested that, at least in the period to the 1974 local government re-organisation, the two levels of party activity were in practice so divorced from one another that the relationship could best be described as one of 'indiffer-ence'.
>
> (p. 10)

This local autonomy did not extend, however, to defying central government when exercising what was seen as its legitimate function expressed through Acts of Parliament, departmental circulars, etc. Indeed councillors saw it as their duty to carry out the intentions behind such 'central direc-tives' but always as interpreted against the needs of Shire. This view, members were keen to point out, was irrespective of the government in power – an important point when, for instance, deciding on matters concerning comprehensive schooling.

Shared Background and Experience

Where did this consensus of views come from if it was not dictated by a clearly stated Conservative policy? Perhaps the values implicit in social class, style of living, accepted social conscience, sense of duty and senior management experience, or a training in one of the major professions, which many councillors had received, all combined to produce a relatively similar world view. An analysis of the background of the sixty councillors prior to 1977, when the majority were still Conservative or Independent, will illustrate this point.

Fourteen were, or had been, in senior management positions in industry and commerce and of these the majority described themselves as company directors. Ten were professionally qualified and described themselves as 'architect', 'consulting engineer', 'accountant', 'solicitor', etc. Seven had senior positions in the Civil Service. Six were landowner-farmers. Eleven described themselves as 'housewives' (although the addresses, and sometimes titles, indicated fairly high social status).

A scan of the names in one year reveals the following 'titles': Commander, Reverend, MP, two lieutenant-colonels, two Ladies, a major, and two JPs.

It was also a relatively old and experienced council. Twenty members were over 60 and forty-five (out of sixty) were over 50. Nearly half had served on the council before. All members served on at least three committees within the council, but their list of outside interests is impressive – usually ranging from about three committees to up to twenty or more. Typical committees included regional planning, nature conservancy, water authority, British Legion housing, family practitioner association, road safety, university council, war pensions, diocesan council and numerous school governorships.

All in all the members had between them considerable and wide-ranging knowledge of, and involvement in, business affairs and local social networks of all kinds. Most had roots in the county, often going back over many generations; they knew it well and shared a common pride in both developing and conserving it.

Furthermore, they knew their officers and referred to a sense of trust and continuity built up over the years. Naturally there was change, but there were always sufficient members and officers spanning more than one period of local government to ensure continuity. This helped create the club-like atmosphere referred to earlier and presented any new member with an already well-formed set of norms and ways of behaving. These had to be learned but once learned they provided a framework of accepted procedures which reduced argument and conflict and expedited business.

One of these unwritten but important norms, mentioned by several members who could look back to the *laissez-faire* period, was that officers should be responsible for initiating and working out the detail of policy, and members should concern themselves only with the 'broad sweep and direction'. The council was, in other words, 'officer led'.

Putting all of these factors together – shared values, steadily growing financial resources, trusted and responsible officers, concern only with policy direction rather than detail, relative autonomy from central government, few, if any, frustrated and vociferous pressure groups and, finally, considerably simpler organizational structures and financial procedures than exist today – it is clear that the role of the councillor in the *laissez-faire* culture was far less stressful, and probably far more enjoyable, than in the periods that were to follow.

But there is another important conclusion to be drawn from this. Policy-making in that time of rapid growth was, by and large, left to the professional officers. If they wished to experiment they would be accorded considerable freedom to do so. There was always accountability but this was not related to clearly defined policy statements based upon explicitly stated long-term goals. The main aim was to grow as quickly as possible along with most other local authorities. This had clear implications for education.

Education in the County

Education departments in local government generally have
gained something of a maverick reputation. They have
always been accorded, and have attempted to maintain, a
high degree of autonomy. Their relationship with central
government through the Department of Education and
Science; their range of functions covering many different
clients with very diverse needs; the provision of numerous
ancillary services including grants, meals, welfare, transport,
etc.; a broad knowledge base calling upon many disciplines
and a lengthy training period for all members of the profession – these factors together set the education department
apart from other departments. Eddison (1975) observes:
'Perhaps the educationists are the most rigid. In many local
authorities with responsibility for education, the education
function has been regarded as almost completely separate
and in many cases even boasted a separate name' (p. 17).
There have, from time to time, even been calls for the
separation of local education management from the rest of
local government.

In terms of its relative autonomy, the education service in
Shire was no exception to this norm. It was always the
biggest spender, accounting for over 60 per cent of the
council's budget, and it has tended to use its funds according
to needs as defined by the education committee and not the
council as a whole. Here some comment on the world of the
officers and the relationship of this world to that of the
members is appropriate.

Senior officers including the chief, deputies, area officers,
advisers and inspectors are professional educationists. Generally they are trained and experienced teachers who have
moved into administration. They know schools as organizations and they know the particular schools and teachers in
their area. They are constantly in touch with national and
local developments in education whether concerned with
curriculum matters, changes in the law, restructuring or new
financial procedures. Within this, their area of professional

competence, educationists assume the right of all professionals, whatever their field, to assess what should count as
sufficient standards of performance in providing a service to
a client group.

The shared professional basis of their knowledge and
experience is reinforced by a physical separation from other
departments. The group work together constantly and share
interests and problems. Over time the department develops
its own norms and values and an accepted set of working
practices. For new members the department, as well as the
profession, provides a socializing environment and a career
structure. It offers a sense of belonging to a group, a clear
working role identity and the perception of being different
from other departments.

These factors – size, complexity, specialized training,
professional orientation and physically separate departmental functioning – together reinforce the autonomy of education in relation to other local government services.

To this 'separatist unit' come elected members as they
take their seat on the education committee. As already
pointed out they bring with them the view that the main
responsibility for policy-making lies with the officers. Their
concern is with broad direction or with particular issues that
might affect their constituents. Their knowledge of education is usually personal – as pupils, parents, or sometimes
governors. It is seldom professional, technical, or, in the
period under review, political. It is largely a 'watchdog'
function allowing the officers to assume control. From this
situation two key figures emerge: the Chief Education
Officer and the Chairman of Education. Their relationship,
which provides the main link between the two worlds, is
crucial.

The power of a Chief Education Officer is formidable, as
Bush and Kogan (1982) have shown, although this power
has changed and possibly diminished as cultures of choice
have become more complex and hostile. In the *laissez-faire*
era, remarks made by Jennings (1977) would almost certainly hold:

Chief education officers seem to delegate few decision-making activities. The flow of information and opinions, the timing or pacing of their presentation and the suggestions for consultation can usually be controlled by the chief education officer.

. . . Interpretation of the Department of Education and Science regulations and of teachers' views and parental reactions is also made by the chief education officer. These presentations can be disputed by members, but members do not often have easy access to information sources.

(p. 46)

This does not make the Chairman of Education supernumerary, far from it, but it does define the role more in terms of a confidant, a trusted ally and a key communicator of ideas and information regarding 'best policies' with, and within, the party group. When issues and problems arise from the members' side it will normally be the chairman who will bring these to the officers. This does not preclude other members from access to officers, particularly with regard to constituency concerns, but generally discussions on major policy matters take place at chief officer–chairman level. Jennings (1977) comments upon the ideal relationship as far as chief officers are concerned:

On the leadership side, chief education officers want chairmen to be interested in and knowledgeable about the service, especially with regard to the magnitude of resources required and the problems to be faced in moving such a massive service. It does not mean detailed understanding of how the service is operated but sufficient knowledge to be confident that the chief education officer and the department are managing the service effectively. Interest should extend far enough to perform the full range of chairmanship duties including the necessary public appearances . . . A chairman who does not get involved in details does the best job of keeping other committee members out of them.

(p. 123)

This view appears to summarize quite well the conditions prevailing in Shire during the *laissez-faire* period. Officers were responsible for steering a fast moving ship with little in the way of maps, an erratic compass and a desire by all concerned to get to a better place as soon as possible. An analogy with the *Mayflower* is hard to resist, but in retrospect, from the perspective of the cuts culture, the *Titanic* has seemed, to some, a better comparison.

The main point is that major policy decisions concerned how to grow and grow quickly. These decisions were made by a few officers within the education department. They were influenced by the mood of the times: the prospect of continuing growth, the popularity accorded to education by the general public and encouragement to experiment with new educational ideas. In this venture they were supported by their councillor partners provided their actions appeared to coincide with the often very loosely perceived needs of the county. For the senior officers in the education service, *laissez-faire* meant relative freedom to pursue their aims, unhindered by outside interference. There were soon to be increasing pressures on this freedom.

5

Planned Growth

It was inevitable that the period of *laissez-faire* would end. Education had become a huge, unwieldy and expensive enterprise. By 1970 it was costing over £2.5 thousand million, equivalent to 7 per cent of gross national income. Its appetite for more funds was insatiable, and its tangible benefits seemed increasingly less attractive and uncertain. The shift towards a planned growth culture, however, was gradual and was caused by three factors: political, organizational and financial. These are considered, briefly, in the national context and then more fully as they affected Shire and other local authorities.

The National Scene

Political Factors
By the mid-1960s the major postwar reconstruction of the system was virtually complete, and the main planks of the 1944 Act were in place, but political parties were beginning to assess the outcomes and to relate them to their own social and economic goals. It was clear that there was a growing divergence of views between the parties as to the best way forward.

The Labour government which took office in 1964 was still committed to expansion but expansion geared towards greater equality of opportunity and, where the need was identified, positive discrimination in favour of under-privileged minorities. To growth, therefore, were added the direction and constraints of political ideology.

Ideologies, certainly as regards education, were influenced by the growth of a relatively new discipline – the 'sociology of education' – which, in some ways, paralleled the emerging 'economics of education' referred to in Chapter 4. The early work of Floud, Halsey and Anderson (1961) and Douglas (1964) was much concerned with inequalities in educational opportunity and attainment. Family background and the internal structure of schools seemed to be the main apparent causes for the 'failure' of working-class children. Official reports were also concerned with the question of 'failure' of certain groups of children and the consequent wastage of talent (Newsom, 1963; Robbins, 1963; Plowden, 1967).

Later, work by Hargreaves (1967) and Lacey (1970) added greater depth to the earlier work and both writers were pessimistic about policies which merely tampered with the system and left basic class inequalities unaffected despite a continuing growth in resources.

The changes which took place from 1964 onwards are well known and well documented from differing perspectives (e.g. Kogan, 1975; Jennings, 1977; Regan, 1977; Mann, 1979; Silver, 1980; CCCS, 1981). The main events were the reorganization of secondary schooling along comprehensive lines and the expansion of further and higher education, in particular the establishment of the polytechnics. There were also moves, embodied in Circulars 11/67 and 19/68, to stimulate investment in educational priority areas and areas suffering 'urban stress'.

The details of these policies, the often controversial values supporting them, and their eventual outcomes are less important here than the fact that a new harder political edge was affecting education. Some form of overall planning, e.g. the submission of reorganization schemes to comply with Circular 10/65, was now becoming necessary.

Money spent on education by local authorities would have to conform, far more than in the past, to priorities laid down by central government.

The Corporate Ideal
The second factor to shift the culture towards one of planned growth was largely organizational and associated with the

desire to achieve what Braybrooke and Lindblom (1970) term 'comprehensiveness' in policy-making. They define this as 'rational choice that responds to a comprehensive consideration of all relevant variables'.

In most organizations, including central and local government, the 'relevant variables' are defined by separate departments or spending units each with its own functions, goals and limited focus. Comprehensiveness, therefore, requires greater co-ordination through appropriate forms of corporate management and planning. In central government the Cabinet, the Treasury, the Public Expenditure Survey Committee (PESC) and after 1970 the Central Policy Review Staff (CPRS) all contributed to the corporate approach.

In the Department of Education and Science (DES) a small planning branch staffed by administrators, economists and statisticians was set up for the first time in 1967. This was expanded and strengthened in 1971 when it became known as the 'department's planning organization' (DPO). A new organizational structure emerged headed by a policy steering group (under the chairmanship of the permanent secretary) and several special policy groups concerned with particular programmes such as schools and higher education. These groups were all serviced by an enlarged planning unit. The intention of this new structure was to provide greater co-ordination and consistency in planning across the DES.

Budgetary Control

Finally, there were a number of moves to introduce greater control over resource allocation through the use of various budgetary instruments. Spiers (1975) and Carley (1980) have catalogued and described the expanding body of 'rational techniques' used in public administration and in policy analysis. These include, for instance, cost-benefit and cost-effectiveness analysis, output budgeting, management by objectives, environmental and social impact assessment, social forecasting, future studies, evaluation research and the use of social or performance indicators.

Underlying them all is a rational procedure which accepts the possibility of determining goals and measuring the extent to which they are achieved. Kirst (1977) summarizes the approach as follows: 'The components of the decision making process include careful elucidation of specific objectives; evaluation of the various alternatives on the basis of their costs and effects; and finally arrival at a value maximising choice' (p. 310). Braybrooke and Lindblom (1970) describe the approach in slightly more cynical terms. To them it represents the ideals of science transferred to the world of values, and this presents problems:

> For on the values side, determination of policy becomes simply a matter of calculation, a question of feeding in the observed facts and thinking consistently through a sequence of logical transformations. One discovers the facts, looks up (or derives) the relevant hypotheticals and deduces by strict logic which policy is to be selected.
>
> (p. 10)

The two main instruments to emerge at the DES in the early 1970s were 'output budgeting' (sometimes referred to as 'programme budgeting' or PPBS) and 'programme analysis and review' (PAR). Both received much publicity at the time but both were abandoned after a few years, leaving behind some valuable lessons regarding the problems and possibilities of the use of such systems in large organizations.

Output budgeting at the DES emanated from the newly formed planning unit and is described in Educational Planning Paper No. 1 (DES, 1970) as:

> a general approach rather than a specific technique. Its specific contribution is to bring together the objectives of a particular service and the resources being devoted to them, and to provide a framework within which the costs and advantages of possible policy choices are examined side by side.

It is a formal system for establishing:

    (i)   what a department is aiming to achieve – what its objectives are – in the areas of policy for which it is responsible;

   (ii) which activities are contributing to these objectives;

  (iii) what resources are being devoted to these activities;

  (iv) what is actually being achieved, or what the outputs are.

(p. 3)

The traditional budget which preceded PPBS relied upon the division of expenditure into a number of fairly standard headings such as teachers' salaries, non-teaching staff, repairs and maintenance, and heating and lighting. These were based upon historical commitments which were adjusted each year according to changed circumstances. The traditional budget was thus unrelated to either specific programmes or to specified aims or objectives for the service as a whole, or to particular parts of it. The programme budget, however, required first the specification of major objectives, then more specific, supporting objectives, then the identification of programmes which contributed towards these major and supporting objectives. The overall budget took on the form of a hierarchy of objectives each related to contributing programmes.

The programmes were each costed and this provided, for the policy-maker, a picture of how resources were allocated according to objectives rather than according to budgetary divisions such as salaries. Furthermore, it was possible to build into the system various evaluative techniques to establish the extent to which objectives were being achieved. Thus the PPBS approach could open the way to, and could incorporate, a range of techniques such as PAR, performance review, cost-effectiveness analysis, and value for money studies.

In practice the scheme proved to be cumbersome; it generated a massive amount of information; it did not fit well with existing organizational divisions; it was expensive to run and, in the end, it failed to attract the commitment of those who were meant to use the information.

It was replaced in 1971 by the more specific PAR system. Its main aims were to bring selected departmental pro- grammes periodically under review, paying specific atten- tion to objectives, outputs and the costs and benefits of alternative ways of achieving them. Lessons learned from the PPBS experience were heeded; particularly that the exercise should involve those who administered the policies.

The new planning unit, using the techniques developed through PAR, produced one of the first and most com- prehensive planning documents to emerge from the DES: the 1972 White Paper *A Framework for Expansion*. The plans were later overtaken by economic events, but this should not obscure the fact that it was an ambitious exercise involving virtually every branch in the department and providing a major reappraisal of all policies within its juris- diction.

Thus, at the national level the culture was changing. The questions being asked were, Where do we want to go and how best can we get there using the resources available as wisely as possible? Local government was also beginning to ask similar questions.

Planned Growth in the County

Shire, like other counties, was faced by the Labour govern- ment's new educational policies, the most important of which was the restructuring of secondary education. But this, as it transpired, posed few major problems in the short term.

Why was it that Shire, a Conservative-dominated auth- ority, so readily accepted planned growth on Labour's terms? The answer is complex, and many reasons have been suggested both by those involved in Shire and by others who have studied the process in other Conservative-led councils. Jennings (1977), for instance, quotes one chief officer as saying: 'Comprehensives came early but not enthusiastically to this county. The landed interests combined with the few

Labourites in a classic seventeenth-century way to defeat the
rising middle class' (p. 100).

But why should 'landed interests', of which Shire had a
fair share amongst its members, so readily follow the comprehensive path? The answer most frequently given by
councillors to whom this question was put was 'because it
seemed best for the children'. They were convinced of the
rightness of the scheme on both organizational and curriculum grounds. Indeed the Conservative chairman (then
deputy chairman) of the education committee wrote a paper
arguing the case for comprehensive schooling.

Against the 'best for the children' argument, however, is a
view from the left which maintains that 'the landed gentry
might be expected to take an objective view on this issue as
their children or grandchildren would be going to private
schools anyway'. Some also argue that there are similarities
between the traditional public school and the comprehensive
in that they both cater for 'mixed ability'.

The party lines were never clearly drawn on the matter. As
Regan (1977) points out, many parents and councillors took
up positions seemingly opposite to those which would have
been expected in terms of right versus left. Feelings for and
against grammar and comprehensive schools were often
more personal than ideological.

Probably, in the end, the pragmatic view held sway. Shire
had much to gain in economic (and probably also improved
curriculum) terms by reorganizing its numerous small rural
secondary schools along comprehensive lines. Whatever the
reasoning, Shire was one of the first counties to introduce
comprehensive schools. This did not end its problems on
this score for, some years later, local government reorganization brought within its structure 'the City'; and here,
against the backcloth of a new Conservative government in
Whitehall and a politically divided council, the issue was to
be fought over in a much more acrimonious way.

Organizational and Budgetary Factors
The politics of planned growth thus came to Shire in a
relatively quiet way, but the transition to a new culture was

brought about more convincingly by the same organizational and budgetary factors discussed earlier at the national
level. In Shire, as in several other authorities, the two factors
were closely interlinked and are here dealt with together.
The new culture was associated mainly with the introduction
of new techniques of budgetary control and with corporate
management. The aim of both was to introduce greater
certainty of direction into the still growing system.

In 1969 the council set up an inter-departmental working
party to consider the feasibility of introducing a PPBS
scheme. A report was submitted to the council in 1971
setting out objectives and programme structures for several
services including education. The report was accepted, and
the working party was instructed to develop it further with
a view to its implementation over a period of years. The
impetus for change was increased as it became clear that local
government reorganization would soon alter the size of the
county and would provide the opportunity for new organizational structures that would facilitate the use of these
planning and budgetary techniques. As a result Shire was
already well advanced in its planning for PPBS and corporate
management by the time local government reorganization
took place in 1974.

Education developed its own programme budget which
was both novel and far reaching. The working party came to
the conclusion that education was not a homogeneous service but rather a conglomeration of separate services including teaching, administration, welfare, catering and transport,
but all, in one way or another, 'geared towards the promotion of the personal development of the individual'.
Within this broad aim it was possible to identify three key
areas called 'scholastic services', 'vocational assistance services' and 'educational and leisure services'. Thus, the general question – what are we doing in education? – was
answered initially in this way. Within these broad areas
more detailed objectives and sub-objectives were derived
and used as the basis for an annual costing exercise.

In addition, the authority, with the encouragement of an
active and progressive County Treasurer (later to become

Chief Executive), became interested in the feasibility of measuring output in education. He reported in 1971:

> It is possible for much time and labour to be expended on assisting people who at the end feel very little helped by the service they have received. Any feeling of having been helped or the reverse is, of course, very personal and subjective and can hardly stand alone as an output measure. Nevertheless, in the absence of any agreement on the criteria, it has been thought worthwhile to gauge the effect of the service by asking those who have received it to say to what extent they have been helped. Measuring the output of the education service in terms of success is an operation of a comparable character to market research: it calls for a continuous process of questioning to find out whether what is being offered in the service is meeting the needs of those to whom it is offered.
>
> An experiment is, therefore, being mounted in the education department to establish whether it is possible to devise and then administer suitable questionnaires for finding the opinion of parents, teachers and pupils about the value (in the light of the cost) of a few strictly limited features of the service offered in the schools.

Shire was thus well advanced in the use of techniques geared towards the development of greater certainty in policy-making by the early 1970s. Furthermore, prior to, and with the advent of, the 1974 local government reorganization Shire moved ahead with its plans for a corporate management system. These were based upon two reports – Maud (1967) and Bains (1972) – which preceded reorganization and strongly espoused the virtues of the corporate approach, particularly as a way of redressing the balance against departmentalism.

The Maud Report stressed the absence of unity in the internal organization of local authorities which, it maintained, was:

> the result of the close association of a particular service, the service committee, the department concerned and the hierar-

chy of professional officers. The separatism of the committees contributes to the separatism of the departments, and
the professionalism of departmental staff feeds upon this
separatism.

(p. 57)

The Bains Report heralded in a new era of corporatism in
which the needs of the community were to be given greater
weight as against the narrower more specific services provided by individual departments.

The reorganization brought with it new co-ordinating
committees, such as the policy and resources committee (to
guide the council in the formulation and co-ordination of its
objectives and priorities, to advise on new and changed
policy and to ensure effective and efficient use of all council
resources); inter-departmental groups and working parties
(to promote co-operation and shared use of resources);
corporate planning teams (to identify and plan for community needs arising in the future and to assess the implications for the council as a whole); performance review
subcommittees (to undertake in-depth studies of particular
services or activities in order to determine the quality of the
performance, the extent to which declared objectives are met
and the more general relevance of the objectives themselves);
and finally and importantly a new tier of overall management
based upon the role of a Chief Executive and supporting
staff.

By 1974 the new structure and the means of achieving
planned growth had been established, but the transition to
this new culture was not easy, nor was it fully operational
when the crisis culture developed shortly afterwards.

In general the corporate approach and the associated
'tools of the trade' were received with mixed feelings by
officers and councillors in most authorities. The problems
which arose were predictable and, perhaps, inevitable. The
task of corporate management was not simply to redress the
balance towards corporatism but to challenge deeply
ingrained attitudes, values and working practices supported
by tradition and strongly rooted professional interests.

Despite resistance, some progress was made, however. Hinings *et al.* (1980), reporting on a study of twenty-seven authorities between 1974 and 1977, indicated a generally favourable attitude amongst chief officers and senior members to the approach, and many instances of inter-departmental co-operation and effective co-ordinating committees were noted. But there were also signs of resistance, apathy and malfunctioning. Below chief officer level, senior officers and their subordinates were less favourably inclined towards corporate management, and many felt totally unaffected by it. Similar views were expressed by rank-and-file councillors and by minority party members. Hinings *et al.* also noted that, by 1977, officers 'seemed rather more willing to accommodate and reconcile within this spectrum of values the ostensibly diverging claims of corporatism and professionalism. There was more realisation that local authorities required, and could encompass, both sets of values' (1980, p. 157).

These views are a fair reflection of the position in Shire in the mid-1970s. But what of education, the normally maverick department – how did it adjust to the pressures to 'join the team'?

Education and Planned Growth

The shift towards corporate management was far from easy for some chief officers even in a time of still expanding resources. The resignation of Avon's chief officer has been described by Bush and Kogan (1982) and his bitter words quoted: 'The management of education is fragmented between so many committees and administrative departments of the Council that there is no united or effective direction of it. The Education Committee cannot exercise that direction, nor can I' (p. 31).

Several writers cite further instances of resistance and suspicion. Bush and Kogan (1982) quote the views of a 'gravely anxious' Society of Education Officers: 'The Society finds it impossible to reconcile the idea of an effective education service within local government with an education committee shorn of the support of a coherent management and advisory service provided by an education department led by a professional CEO' (p. 32).

Regan (1977) quotes Lord Alexander, writing in *Education* in February 1974, as follows:

> It may be that education looms so large in local government that those concerned with other services are naturally jealous of the resources which have to be voted to education, and this no doubt leads to a strong desire to support what is now called 'corporate management' so that all those in local government who are not concerned with education may bring pressure to bear to exercise a tighter control on the education service.
>
> (p. 207)

Nevertheless there were those such as Birley in Liverpool and Aitken in Coventry for whom there were no such fears and they became deeply involved in the council's corporate plans. In Shire the Chief Education Officer had noted the problem of a dual, and potentially conflicting, role: that of head of a department and a member of a corporate team which may sometimes wish to shift the balance of resources away from education. But prior to the full effects of the cuts being felt in the late 1970s no serious conflicts arose – a view confirmed by other members of the team.

The reorganization and the considerable efforts put into the establishment of corporate working, however, had caused further development of the programme budget to be postponed and, as it turned out, eventually cancelled. It was used for five years alongside the traditional budget but it was clear that it would demand considerable work each year and it had not proved popular with members. It did leave behind, though, a legacy of ideas about planning and the acceptance of procedures relating to the statement of objectives and the costing of alternative plans of action (option budgeting). These were continued and were later to prove useful as the culture changed once more.

In summary, therefore, it was possible over the period beginning in the late 1960s to perceive a change in the approach to policy-making both at national and local level and, in particular, in connection with education. General aims were being formulated and questioned. Outcomes were emerging from the *laissez-faire* period and were being compared, often unfavourably, to expectations. Central government began to develop an ideological commitment towards certain approaches to education and it was prepared to impose these upon local government.

New forms of organizational structures and means of budgetary control were also introduced which attempted to provide more comprehensiveness and certainty in the policy-making process.

In Shire the club-like atmosphere remained for councillors. It was still a pleasant place to spend part of one's time and energy. The generally shared goal of developing secondary education along comprehensive lines was both exciting and fulfilling for most members, particularly those on the education committee. The new corporate structures did not seem to have a major impact on day-to-day interactions, since the view of an officer-led council still prevailed. Many members did not fully understand the new budgetary programmes but as these did not replace the existing more familiar procedures they were able to let well alone. Planned growth, for the majority, meant a greater sense of purpose but no immediate added responsibility nor conflict.

At officer level there were changes to adjust to. The sense of autonomy and relative departmental isolation were beginning to break down. There was no immediate threat since the 'cake' was still growing, and each department could still expect an increasing share. But there was more complexity in the negotiations; more meetings to attend; more people to convince and generally more interaction outside of the department.

This was not altogether bad. A wider view was obtained, and more people became acquainted with each other. Overall, the culture became marginally more cohesive and less fragmented. Corporate goals became more prominent, and departmental aims had to be examined against these. But the culture did not have time to develop; it was overtaken by events – the advent of crisis.

Before turning to the main part of the book dealing with crisis and cuts it is worth repeating the point that the shift from growth to contraction was traumatic in its effects. It smote hard at deeply ingrained attitudes based upon notions of continuing growth which, as Stewart (1983a) notes, 'were important formative influences on the working of local government . . . written into the working experiences of most officers and of many councillors' (p. 42).

Perhaps the most illuminating statement of all came from the Society of Education Officers (SEO, 1974) which, looking back over the five years since 1969, pointed to certain ominous changes in the annual White Papers on public expenditure:

> These show: (a) that the overall rate of expansion for public expenditure has been reduced (3% in the 1969 White Paper; 2.3% in 1971; 2.5% in 1972; 2% in 1973); and (b) that the rate of growth for education has been changed relative to other services; for example health and social services. (For education 3.8% in 1969; 4.5% in 1971; 5.0% in 1972; and 4.8% in 1973, compared with 3.8%, 5.1% and 4.6% for health and social services.) . . . translated to local level, this situation is posing some fierce problems for local authorities.
>
> (p. 6)

It is a salutary reminder of the changes which took place later that, in 1974, a slight slowing down of the rate of growth to 4.8 per cent was providing 'fierce problems'. The problems which were soon to emerge made what in 1974 had seemed 'fierce' appear positively benign.

6

The Crisis Culture (1): Contraction

Habermas (1976) suggests that crises arise when 'the structure of a social system allows fewer possibilities for problem solving than are necessary for the continued existence of the system' (p. 2). He continues by stressing the subjective nature of crisis: 'Thus, only when members of a society experience structural alterations as critical for continued existence and their social identity threatened can we speak of crisis' (p. 3).

A crisis, therefore, exists if enough people can be persuaded that it exists. The analysis of crisis is concerned with how individuals and groups perceive and respond to events, as well as with the events themselves. This study is concerned with both.

Herman (1973) suggests three essential elements of crisis: threat involving a potential hindrance to an important organizational state or goal; short decision-time; and an element of surprise. These ideas have been further developed by Billings, Milburn and Schaalman (1980), who suggest the following key concepts.

(1)   Triggering and sensing: a triggering event must be perceived, attended to and evaluated against how things should be.

(2)   Crisis definition: this involves valuing possible losses and estimating the probability of loss. Low probability and small potential losses will not promote the triggering event to the status of crisis. There is, however, always the possibility of individuals or groups seeking to influence the views of others in order to affect their assessment of the situation.

Another important element is the degree of uncertainty about the kind of response that should be made to the triggering event. If, despite high probability of an event occurring coupled with potentially high losses, an effective (and preferably routine) response is available, the event will not be defined as a crisis.

(3)   Time pressure: Herman suggests that 'Without time pressure a problem will be left to the future and systematically mis-perceived. The more distant a future negative consequence the less negative it will seem.' Pressure on the time available to find solutions often causes the most stressful kind of crisis perception. The decision-maker feels that losses will occur if action is not taken, but there is not sufficient time to prepare a satisfactory response.

The element of surprise is not specifically mentioned in the above analysis but it is implicit in the notion of response uncertainty. Response uncertainty can be lessened through pre-planning. It may not be the unexpectedness of the event itself which leads to perceived crises but the lack of contingency planning. Contingency planning in the face of potential enforced economies is one element that may help an organization move from a crisis culture to a cuts culture as described in later chapters.

The three elements of crisis – triggering event, crisis definition and time pressure – fit well with the dimension of a crisis culture as defined by the matrix on page 39. The triggering event which provides the hindrance to an important organization state is *contraction* and the crisis definition and short decision-time are closely associated with the element of *uncertainty*. The present chapter is concerned with contraction, and the next with uncertainty.

Local Government in Contraction

Public expenditure by central and local government has increased steadily since 1950 whether measured in current prices, real terms (adjusting for inflation), or as a percentage of the gross national product. Between 1950 and 1981 this percentage rose from 34.9 to 47.0. Successive governments have attempted to control this growth.

Traditionally about two-thirds of local government income has come from central government in the form of rate support and other subsidies and direct grants. The remainder was raised mainly on local taxes – the rates. A local authority's budget was normally based upon historical patterns of expenditure for each service, to which was added increments for annual growth. There was always a certain flexibility in this procedure in so far as rates could be increased to meet extra expenditure, and also a degree of stability in that government contributions could be expected to keep pace with the increases on roughly a 'two-thirds to one-third' sharing basis.

'The cuts' are the result of substantial changes in this process. First, central government has steadily reduced its overall contribution via the rate support grant from over 60 per cent to under 50 per cent between 1974 and 1985. To give some indication of the extent of the reductions involved for 1985, figures for a few shire counties are set out in Table 6.1.

The Association of Metropolitan Authorities estimated that twenty-nine out of thirty-nine shire counties would suffer in the latest round of cuts at the start of 1985. The reasoning behind the cuts also confounded many

Table 6.1 *Losses as a result of reductions in rate support grant 1985/86*

County	Loss (£m)
Berkshire	£10.4 (18.55%)
Gloucestershire	£3.2 (4.5%)
Essex	£19 (12.58%)
Hampshire	£15.5 (8.29%)
Surrey	£15.7 (17.5%)

Source: The Times, 13 December 1984.

authorities, for there appeared to be no logic determining what one authority should bear in relation to another.

Local authorities wishing to maintain levels and standards of service since the cuts began nearly a decade ago have had either to find alternative ways of raising the money or to devise more efficient methods of working.

Responses have varied. Many authorities have sought some savings through more 'efficient' operations and have reduced manpower totals accordingly. Caulcott (1983) notes an overall reduction in full-time equivalent employees of 2.9 per cent between 1977 and 1982, although this is not spread evenly between services, and education has taken a larger reduction amounting to about 6 per cent. Some authorities have increased charges for various services in order to generate more income, and school meals provide a typical example of a generally slow but steady rise in price. In theory it might also be considered possible for an authority to maintain its level of services for a short time by calling upon its reserves or balances. This would clearly depend upon the level of balances available but would normally not be acceptable as other than a temporary solution.

Even taken together these three measures – improved efficiency, increased charges, and calls upon balances – could not keep up with the decline in central government support. Local authorities were, therefore, forced to look towards increased income from rates. Here, however, they were to meet further problems.

Most Conservative councillors were pledged to contain or reduce rates and many felt that they had been elected on that understanding. But more importantly, the government was committed to reduce public spending and to lower inflation. Increases in rates would run counter to both of these aims, and councils were strongly discouraged from adopting this solution.

To ensure compliance, the government introduced a cash limits system later accompanied by spending targets for each authority. These were backed by a penalty system which in effect fined authorities which exceeded their target. This was effective as a constraint on most authorities, particularly those with a Conservative majority, but to put the final seal on the possibility of using the 'rates solution' the government introduced the controversial 'rate capping' Bill in December 1983 which reached Parliament in 1985. Most authorities are therefore squeezed between reduced central government support on the one hand and the difficulty, on the other, of recouping their loss by the traditional method of increasing the rates.

As far as 'sensing the triggering event' was concerned there was certainly plenty of warning as to what might be expected. Election manifestos, ministerial statements, government circulars and White Papers all provided formal indicators of intention to control spending. These indications were reinforced, formally and informally, on networks such as the Association of County Councils, the Association of Municipal Authorities and the Consultative Council for Local Government Finance. There were adequate cues for sensing an emerging problem.

Shire in Contraction

We began the study of Shire by considering the effects of the cuts upon the schools. It was clear that the service had suffered both physically and psychologically and that, although it could be described as 'coping', the damage caused by a continual paring down of support services was having a cumulative negative effect. Here we look at the contracting situation in Shire, particularly regarding its education service, that led to the problems described.

By the mid-1970s the omens for the forthcoming crisis should have been clear. In retrospect it seems that there were enough 'triggering events' to alert the policy-makers to the dangers ahead. But those involved in Shire might be forgiven for not taking the matter too seriously. After all, there had been many problems before, as central government applied the financial brakes, but these had usually been successfully overcome.

The stop–go of Whitehall intervention in local spending

had had a long history under both Labour and Conservative administrations. The County Treasurer recalled the problems created by the Wilson government as far back as 1968 when there was no increase in the rate support grant despite high inflation. The Chief Education Officer remembered the so-called 'Barber cuts' of 1973 which were seen then as 'a useful pruning exercise'.

Else and Marshall (1981) refer to more recent developments as 'the unplanning of public expenditure'. In a detailed paper analysing the introduction of 'cash limits' they show how Labour between 1976 and 1979 tightened, eased and then re-tightened controls on local spending.

It was, perhaps, not unreasonable, therefore, for some officers and members to assume that present difficulties were no more than a temporary set-back. Events, however, eventually began to prove them wrong. As the council was expected, sometimes more than once in a year, to find substantial savings, the feeling of crisis began to grow.

The effects of the cuts on the annual expenditure in Shire are best illustrated by reference to the 'Report of the County Treasurer' which is submitted to the council each January and contains details of government guidelines or restrictions on expenditure for the coming year. The need for savings became a constant theme in the treasurer's report from 1977 onwards. The following extracts will provide the flavour.

The total increase in estimated net expenditure for the current year is £5,258,000 which is barely 11% over the original budget.

(1975/6)

. . . expenditure for the current year is expected to be very close to the original estimates, the rate of growth for 1976/77 has been reduced overall to 0.4%.

(1976/7)

This virtually marked the end of growth. New stringent measures were imposed by the government during the year.

The settlement for 1977/78 reduced the grant . . . by about £5 million and fixed cash limits which will probably mean a further reduction in real terms because inflation continues to run at a high rate. (Retail price index to November 15%.)

(1977/8)

In summary, our share of the needs element of the grant has dropped yet again, this time by £889,000; the transport supplementary grant has been cut by £404,000; the resources grant taken back in the current year is £1.3 million.

(1979/80)

In the current year the revised estimates include savings of £2.5 million and for 1980/81 estimates have been reduced by 1% in real terms plus the equivalent of commitments to produce an overall reduction of £2.4 million.

(1980/1)

The reductions in expenditure in real terms are equivalent to 3% which is in line with the Government's requirements for 1981/82. The total is £6.7 million excluding redundancy payments.

(1981/2)

Thus, the cuts have continued year by year with increasing severity. There has been no let-up, and in 1985 Shire was one of the counties required to adapt to a further reduction in the rate support grant. Estimates vary as to the overall amount of the savings made (and much depends upon how savings and cuts are defined), but it would seem that since 1977 the figure is in excess of £20 million.

Within this contracting situation education has been required to make its contribution to the savings, and this is considered next.

Education in Contraction

Education, as the largest spender in local authorities, has been at the forefront of the cuts. It would, as a service, have suffered anyway as local authorities shared out responsibility for savings across departments; but in addition, the decline in the birth rate some years earlier brought falling rolls to primary schools and paved the way for further cuts in the education budget. Furthermore, as the economy, the main plank in the growth culture, declined there were more general repercussions affecting confidence and traditional assumptions about the nature, direction and value of growth.

There may be an analogy between the changing cultures discussed here and the human life cycle. The optimism and flexibility of youth (*laissez-faire*) give way to a more responsible and cautious attitude as individuals mature (planned growth), but this is sometimes followed by what is popularly known as a 'mid-life crisis' involving a loss of confidence and a questioning of identity and previous actions.

Education was beginning to face a similar loss of confidence as the growth culture came to an end. What was education for? What had it done to improve individuals or society? Was life better in 1974 than it was twenty years earlier despite considerable increases in expenditure? Had any of the innovations provided effective and efficient ways of organizing the service? Were not the traditional ways of doing things perhaps better after all?

For many observers, not least those who were to gain control of central policy-making and financing, these questions were mostly answerable in a way not favourable to the existing state of the art. The education service, therefore, faced problems on three fronts: economic contraction as a national ailment; falling rolls affecting the size of the operation; and a serious drop in confidence related to what education could, or should, be expected to do.

Before considering educational contraction in Shire, however, it will be useful to place it in the wider national perspective.

The National Scene
Education is a service which over nearly three decades has witnessed steady growth in terms not only of increasing numbers of pupils but also of improvements in the extent and quality of the provision. The 1950s and 1960s marked an

era of confidence in education as an important contributor to economic and social welfare. By the mid-1970s, however, the position was beginning to change, and education was increasingly being called to account.

Total expenditure, which in real terms had steadily grown for almost two decades, contracted and then levelled out after 1976.

The figures indicate that, in real terms, total expenditure on education is now less than it was in 1975/6. Education has taken its share of the cuts nationally.

The contraction of the service is further indicated by staffing levels in the teaching force. Walsh *et al.* (1984) note that between 1979 and 1982 there was a fall of 21,000 in the number of teachers which is equivalent to 5 per cent of the total force. Projections indicate further falls (DES, 1985) and in April 1985 a survey by *The Times Educational Supplement* of local authorities suggested that over 7,000 teaching posts in secondary schools would be shed in the coming year. (*TES* 1985.)

Despite the efforts of those employed within the education service to use the falling rolls situation to reduce the pupil teacher ratio the government implemented a policy of making corresponding reductions in the teaching force. In fact the 1981 White Paper on Public Expenditure refers to 'some slight tightening of staffing standards', resulting in a marginal worsening of the pupil–teacher ratio. However, as the school population began to change from 1980 towards a higher proportion of relatively more expensive secondary pupils the effect of this policy presented even greater problems for those managing the service. The government subsequently relaxed their policy and there was a slight improvement in the P–TR from 18.3:1 in 1982 to 17.9:1 in 1985 (DES, 1985, p. 46).

Government control of local education expenditure, however, is still indirect despite recent measures to influence the amounts spent and the number of teachers employed. A sum for education is included in the block grant paid to each authority each year and according to the Department of the Environment's guidelines (DOE, 1980).

Table 6.2 Total expenditure on education (in £ billion)

	1970/1	1976/7	1977/8	1978/9	1979/80	1980/1	1981/2	1982/3	1983/4
Actual	2.2	6.4	6.6	7.4	8.6	10.5	11.4	12.2	12.8
At 1982/3 prices	10.1	13.7	12.4	12.6	12.5	12.9	12.7	12.8	12.8
At 1970/1 = 100	100	136	123	125	125	128	126	127	127

Sources: DES Statistical Bulletin; Finance 10/84. Updated by DES Statistics Department (Extn. 9132) September 1985.

> The size of any individual service component . . . for any
> authority gives no indication of what that authority should
> spend on the service. It is simply a contribution to the
> authority's overall GRE (grant related expenditure). The
> level at which an authority spends in relation to that overall
> GRE and the way in which it divides the money it has
> between services is a matter for that authority alone.
>
> (p. 3)

Thus, despite increasing government controls on both the
amount of local government expenditure and central policies
which seek to influence the way money is spent, local
authorities still retain a certain measure of freedom and this
is illustrated by pupil–teacher ratios ranging from 16:1 to
25:1 in primary schools and from 12:1 to 17:1 in secondary
schools in different authorities (HMI, 1985).

Education in Shire
There are a number of problems involved in establishing the
extent and nature of the cuts in Shire. Financial, numerical
and descriptive indicators all suggest a general contraction of
the education service. But, first, what is a cut and what is
contraction?

Clearly cuts and contraction imply reductions but reductions in what? The difficulty is in establishing a consistent
base upon which to calculate the reductions. For example,
suppose the annual expenditure on education has steadily
increased over a number of years and for the coming year
was expected to rise by, say, £6 million or about 10 per cent.
Then, due to external constraints £3 million was cut from the
budget limiting the rise to 5 per cent. Is this a contraction?

The matter is further complicated by resource re-allocation. Authorities are continually facing demands for new
commitments, sometimes of a statutory nature, and it may
be that the only way they see to meet these demands is to find
savings in other parts of the budget. Supposing that growth
were to remain the same as in the above example, i.e. up by
10 per cent, but that an increase in the further education
sector is offset by reductions in primary and secondary
schooling. In this case new commitments appearing in an

overall statement of expenditure will mask reductions in other parts.

There are other factors which may also affect the base line. School reorganization plans, for instance, which are generally not directly concerned with savings, may affect the budget in any one year quite considerably. But perhaps the major extraneous factor is falling rolls. Fewer pupils can mean fewer classrooms, fewer schools and, most importantly from a financial point of view, fewer teachers. Such factors must be taken into account when interpreting financial statements.

Then there is the question of income. Should expenditure be dealt with as a gross or a net item? Some income is obtained from other authorities that use Shire's educational services. Also, the sale of school meals and drinks provides funds, and these are sometimes increased by external grants such as the EEC subsidy on milk. Government grants are also available to cover mandatory awards for teacher training and further and higher education. The pooling system for expenditure on advanced further education can provide another source of funds if the authority has earned a net credit. A relatively small income also comes from fees, accommodation, transport, etc. All of these vary from year to year and alter the base, even if only marginally.

Finally there is the problem of inflation. Expenditure in one year can be compared with that in another in real terms only if an adjustment for increased prices is made. Indices for this purpose are produced from time to time – by the DES and the Chartered Institute of Public Finance and Accountancy (CIPFA) – but due to the different rates of inflation for different goods and services such indices are inevitably estimations.

The result of all of these problems is that financial statements, comparing expenditure over a period of years, can be taken only as a possible indicator of contraction (or growth) in the service. Each statement must be interpreted taking into account the factors mentioned above.

In the rest of this chapter the evidence will be dealt with in two parts. The first will be concerned mainly with financial and numerical indicators such as overall annual expenditure, unit costs and pupil–teacher ratios. The second part will be largely descriptive and will analyse the kind of cuts made and the parts of the service affected.

Financial Indicators of Contraction   In terms of gross and net expenditure at constant prices, i.e. making allowance for inflation, Shire began to contract in 1980. This is shown in Table 6.3.

Table 6.3   *Gross and net expenditure at constant prices 1974–82*

	Gross (£m)	At 1982 prices (£m)	% change	Net (£m)	At 1982 prices (£m)	% change
1974/5	43.3	117.9		38.6	105.4	
1975/6	56.7	122.5	3.9	49.1	106.1	0.7
1976/7	63.3	124.7	1.8	54.5	107.4	1.2
1977/8	69.3	126.8	1.7	58.2	106.5	−0.8
1978/9	78.5	131.1	3.4	64.9	108.3	1.6
1979/80	89.1	131.8	0.5	74.0	109.5	1.1
1980/1	104.9	122.7	−6.9	87.9	103.7	−5.3
1981/2	113.9	119.8	−2.4	95.4	101.1	−2.5
1982/3	118.7	118.7	−0.9	99.5	99.5	−1.5

Source: Shire annual expenditure statistics, adjusted for inflation using CIPFA ready reckoner.

These figures indicate a steady, if erratic, fall in expenditure over nearly a decade. They do, however, include the steadily falling rolls situation which began in 1976 and is still continuing. The extent of the fall is apparent from Table 6.4.

Table 6.4   *Pupil numbers in thousands*

	Primary	Secondary	Total
1975	52.0	38.7	90.7
1978	48.5	41.8	90.3
1981	44.3	41.8	86.1
1984	39.6	39.2	78.8
1985	39.4	38.1	77.5

Source: Shire annual school statistics.

Government policy requires authorities to match falling numbers with reduced expenditure. Shire, a county which normally follows government guidelines, should therefore show a fall in overall expenditure, and this was demonstrated in Table 6.3. But to establish whether there has been contraction over and above that associated with falling rolls it is necessary to look at other indicators.

Unit costs, if adjusted for inflation, should show the extent to which spending per child has varied over the years. A rise would indicate that some of the savings from falling rolls were being used to improve quality, and a fall would suggest an added level of contraction. The figures are set out in Table 6.5.

Table 6.5   *Annual unit costs per pupil 1974–83*

	Primary £	At 1982/3 prices £	Secondary £	At 1982/3 prices £
1974/5	212	579	366	980
1975/6	274	587	448	981
1976/7	302	597	490	968
1977/8	330	606	526	965
1978/9	370	621	577	967
1979/80	428	635	634	940
1980/1	530	627	819	970
1981/2	603	639	939	996
1982/3	657	657	1,001	1,001

Source: Shire annual expenditure statistics, adjusted for inflation using CIPFA ready reckoner.

The first point to note is that the figures, adjusted for inflation, remain relatively constant over the years. In the secondary sector the expenditure per child is almost the same in 1974 as in 1982. There is, however, an increase on the primary side and this needs some explanation. To appreciate the situation it is necessary to look at the trend in pupil–teacher ratios – see Table 6.6.

Table 6.6   *Pupil–teacher ratios 1974–84*

	Primary	Secondary
1974/5	23.90	17.90
1978/9	23.29	17.27
1980/1	22.94	17.35
1982/3	23.28	17.32
1983/4	23.10	17.25

Source: Shire annual school statistics.

The most noticeable point is how little change there has been, and where change has occurred it has been for the better. In both primary and secondary sectors the pupil–teacher ratio is marginally better in 1984 than it was in 1974. This would not be remarkable were it not for the fact that falling rolls, particularly among largely rural, small schools, make the maintenance of a stable ratio extremely difficult without increasing unit costs. It is this which probably accounts for the rise in primary school unit costs in 1981 (Table 6.5).

Shire had over 300 primary schools in the 1970s although this fell to 284 in 1981 and 276 in 1983. In 1983 nearly 20 per cent of these schools had less than fifty pupils, and 40 per cent had less than a hundred. The difference that this makes to costs is indicated by the following figures, taken from Shire's annual booklet, *School Statistics* (1983): cost per pupil in a small school (average number of pupils: 31) is £913.50; in a medium-sized school (average number of pupils: 142) it is £484; and in a large school (average number of pupils: 330) it is £460.50.

The fall in unit cost of nearly 100 per cent in moving from small to medium size is dramatic and is of particular concern to an authority which has about 40 per cent of its primary pupils in the higher cost bracket. The 1983 statistics show that nearly 70 per cent of children are taught in groups of less than thirty, and 12 per cent in classes of less than twenty.

The conclusion to be drawn from the fact that relatively

high cost primary schools have been preserved against a background of falling rolls and financial stringency is that other parts of the service have suffered disproportionately. This point is taken up again later.

Again, in the secondary sector, the stability in cost per pupil and the slight fall in the pupil–teacher ratio is interesting. What it suggests is that the same amount of money, in real terms, and the same teaching input are still available to each child as was the case about a decade earlier. This is largely due to the formula used to calculate staffing in the schools – a formula designed to protect schools from the uneven short-term effects of falling rolls. The 'curriculum model', as it is called, is discussed in more detail later but its effect, in parallel with the protection of the staffing ratios in the primary schools, was to divert the cuts elsewhere, mainly to the various support services.

The protection of staffing ratios did not mean that teachers were not shed from the establishment. As numbers of pupils fell the teaching force also fell more or less in proportion. The reduction, however, largely was achieved by natural wastage, early retirement and voluntary redundancy. This affected mainly those teachers at the higher end of the salary scales. The contracting nature of the service also meant the recruitment of fewer new teachers in the lower salary range.

Statistics already indicate a growing proportion of older teachers, particularly in the primary sector where 60 per cent are over 40. The figure is lower in the secondary sector (just over 40 per cent) but this is expected to increase as the effects of falling rolls are felt over a longer period. This is in line with government forecasts for the country as a whole (DES, 1983a).

This is an important point in assessing the implications of the financial statistics discussed earlier. If, as seems to be the case, the age drift is upwards, then a constant unit cost per pupil, coupled with a stable pupil–teacher ratio, means that the relative cost of the teacher input, as against other items of expenditure (such as learning materials and support services), is increasing. Savings, therefore, if they have to be made, must come from somewhere other than teachers' salaries and, as the age profile of the teaching force moves upwards, more savings in non-teacher items of expenditure will be demanded. The question then becomes, What else can 'reasonably' be cut?

Judicious Pruning   The choice of where to cut is far from easy. As was shown earlier, the policy which emerged was based upon the clear premise that the roots and main stem of the service (curriculum, teachers, and pupil–teacher ratios) should be preserved, and that savings should be made through 'judicious pruning' (a term used by a councillor not opposed to the cuts) of minor branches. The analogy might be extended one stage further by noting that peripheral growths are more easily trimmed away with less effort than the major ones; as in horticulture, the result might be regarded by some as an improvement in appearance as well as leaving room for new growths of a different kind to emerge in the future.

Cuts made in this way can be identified from committee papers. They appear as specified items of expenditure which will not be incurred in the following year. Overall, between 1976 and 1983 they amounted to approximately £9.5 million. Of this sum, roughly £8 million was directly or indirectly associated with primary and secondary schooling.

Although it is not possible to state exactly the savings made as a result of falling rolls, an estimate based upon figures for school closures and consequent direct staff reductions, coupled with an approximate 2 per cent cut in the teaching force described later, suggests an amount of approximately £2 million. This leaves something like £6 million saved from other sources, the majority of which were not associated with the full-time teaching force.

Whereas the total savings of £9.5 million represent only about 1 per cent of total education expenditure over the seven-year period, the £6 million saved by pruning the schooling budget is closer to 10 per cent of non-teacher expenditure on primary and secondary schools during the same period.

If teachers, their pupils and curriculum activities form the roots, stem and essential life of the educational plant, then the branches and foliage which support, sustain and enrich the system are the physical environment, teaching support services and equipment, non-curricular services for pupils and their families, and special activities such as sport and music. It is in these four areas that the majority of the savings were made, and they are dealt with in turn.

The Physical Environment   Perhaps this is one of the most obvious areas to look to for savings. Regular maintenance is generally considered to be good policy from every point of view, but the norms and standards which govern maintenance are not immutable. Whether a building should be painted every five, seven or ten years depends upon many factors such as position, amount of wear experienced and type of construction. There is much room for flexibility.

Not all grass has to be cut regularly. Cleaning can be more carefully controlled in terms of both what is cleaned and when. Furniture and equipment can also, if necessary, be made to last that little bit longer. Shoddiness and dowdiness, despite their physical unattractiveness, are tolerable. The opening of newly completed buildings, whilst looked forward to, can generally be delayed; the system has, after all, managed without them previously. This will result in a saving in recurrent as well as capital costs.

Over a period of seven years the savings made under this heading amount to about £250,000 (about 0.4 per cent of total non-teacher expenditure over the period). But this may not represent the real cut, for once cutting is built into the annual budgetary system the attitude can soon prevail that there is little point in putting into the estimates such 'non-essential' items as painting, for they will only have to be taken out again later.

Another aspect of the physical environment which demands considerable resources is heating. Any cost-conscious administrator will look to this area for possible savings and, indeed, as many well-advertised energy conservation schemes have shown, the potential is considerable. Shire saved £230,000 (0.3 per cent of total non-teacher expenditure) on fuel bills over the period.

Teaching Support Teachers do not act alone. They are supported in various ways by other people such as assistants, supply teachers, peripatetic specialists, advisers, clerical and adminstrative personnel, and by teaching resources in the form of books, materials and equipment. Furthermore, as they are expected to improve their teaching and update their work, facilities are provided under the general heading of in-service education and training and also teacher's centres where they can meet locally to discuss specific issues. All of these supports provide potential for trimming and over the years have been treated accordingly.

Approximately £1.5 million (2.5 per cent of total non-teacher expenditure) was saved under this heading. A few examples of the cuts will indicate the nature of the savings:

  books, materials and equipment – £604,000;
  nursery/welfare assistance – £516,000;
  central office and advisory staff – £137,000;
  in-service training and teacher centres – £123,000;
  supply teachers – £93,000;
  clerical assistance – £76,000.

Not all of these cuts were made at once, and in most cases the total was built up over several years.

Non-Curricular Services This heading covers a number of items including meals and milk, transport and road crossings, clothing allowances and assistance with boarding fees. It is in this area that education begins to enter the welfare field. It engages in the kind of services and assistance which some councillors feel is beyond its basic functions – although such a view would be considered controversial.

Of all the cuts in this area the school meals service has proved to be the most productive. In this respect it is worth quoting from a report by the Chief Education Officer to the new council in 1981:

> The 1980 Education Act gave authorities complete flexibility to determine both the content and price of the meal. As a result of a major reorganisation of the School Meals Service, reducing staffing levels, closing down kitchens and a change in menus to achieve lower food costs, the level of subsidy to the School Meals Service has been more than halved in two years to an expected figure of around £2.8m.

Overall, between 1976 and 1983, savings on meals (including increased charges), milk and lunchtime supervision amounted to over £3.2 million.

Further savings were made by reducing transport facilities to and from school and levying new or increased charges. There was also the controversial elimination of road crossing patrols (later, partially reinstated as a result of protest action by parents). Together, savings in these two areas amounted to about £100,000.

Other smaller sums amounting to about £20,000 were culled from the clothing and uniform budget and from assistance with independent school fees.

Special Activities   Where the 'essential' curriculum ends, and extra or voluntary activities begin, is a difficult question. Should music, swimming and environmental studies in field centres be regarded as essential or otherwise? Shire either cut back the facilities in these areas or began to charge for them, and although the amounts received were not large they proved useful additions to the overall savings necessary to meet the target set.

A number of field centres were also closed or reorganized. These moves, together with those mentioned above, brought the total savings under this heading to about £260,000 and the total under the four areas to roughly £6 million.

The Reduction in the Teaching Force   In setting the annual target for each authority, the government allows a percentage increase on the basic figure for wage settlements in the coming year. In its attempt to control inflation this percentage has generally been kept to a low figure – 3 or 4 per cent. If wage settlements exceed this figure the authority concerned must either find compensatory savings elsewhere or run the risk of financial penalties.

In 1981 the Burnham settlement for teachers' salaries exceeded the amount included in the target and the amount set aside in Shire's annual budget. Perhaps this could have been predicted but, as was its policy, the council adhered strictly to government guidelines in setting the budget. The result was that the education service was required to reduce expenditure by nearly £1 million in other ways in order to finance the increase.

The solution adopted was to reduce the size of the teaching force by about a hundred teachers. A note in the annually produced *School Statistics* shows a fall from 1,945 to 1,797 teachers (full time equivalents) and comments: 'The number of teachers has reduced in accordance with the staffing scale and pupil decline but the change between 1981 and 1982 also incorporates the 2% reduction made for the 1981/82 academic year.' This was a highly controversial decision and went against a firm pledge to protect the curriculum and the relative size of the teaching establishment. Several unsuccessful attempts were subsequently made by some councillors to reinstate this particular saving.

Terms used to describe the cuts, by Conservative as well as opposition councillors, have included 'irritating', 'tardy', 'penny-pinching', 'frustrating' and 'in the long run, downright bad for the service'. These views would certainly be echoed by officers.

To summarize, it seems that all indicators, despite their complexity, point to contraction of local government spending over the last decade; and within local authorities, education has borne its share of the cuts. In Shire, whatever indicators are used, they point to the fact that the service has contracted in real terms over and above the savings produced by falling rolls. These cuts, in large part, account for the effects on the schools described in Chapters 2 and 3. The cuts are not great in their magnitude and they have largely left the staffing ratios intact, but the continual paring down of the supporting fabric of the system has led to a clear weakening of the service both physically and psychologically.

We now turn to an examination of the process which lay behind and led up to this position. It took place in conditions of extreme uncertainty.

7

The Crisis Culture (2): Uncertainty

This chapter is concerned with the second main element in the crisis culture: uncertainty and its corollaries, defensiveness, shift in power and lowered morale. It is in this respect that crisis definition and the subjective views of those involved become important. The chapter is in two parts. The first deals with uncertainty at the national level and the second with Shire and uncertainty.

General uncertainty

The initial major uncertainty surrounded government intentions towards local authorities. There was general agreement that the government did intend to take measures to control spending; it had been done in the past, although the action taken was regarded by many as tinkering rather than serious interference. What was not known was the extent of the likely measures nor whether the government would be prepared to risk losing popularity, particularly amongst its own supporters on local councils, by imposing more than token restraints. There were many who thought that it would not, that a slowing down of growth was all that was expected and that this would be both desirable and acceptable.

Again, although the need for haste was often a factor in making cuts, there were generally certain items in the budgets of most councils such as capital expenditure, new projects, maintenance of buildings or repayment of loans which could be deferred and thereby create a breathing space. With these as possible targets for delay there might be inconvenience and frustration but not crisis. Problems of this kind had occurred in the past and been adequately and routinely dealt with – why not again?

This time, however, it was different. In Shire from 1979 onwards (admittedly some time after their Labour counter-parts and many senior officers) some Conservative council-lors were using the term 'crisis'. But the crisis was not quite the same as the acute form suggested by Billings, Milburn and Schaalman (1980) and discussed in Chapter 6. As per-ceived by those in local government, it was brought about mainly by two factors: persistence and uncertainty. This combination produced a situation which differs from those normally thought of as crises.

Jackson (1976), for instance, analyses a series of events including floods, hurricanes, riots, mine disasters, pollution, police strikes and kidnappings. Such crises are normally one-off events and are themselves limited in time. The situation facing local government, however, was more of an extended, intermittent nature, causing 'reeling' rather than collapse.

The unexpectedness was not associated with suddenness, for there had been many warnings, but with persistence and a multitude of novel constraining measures for which no contingency plans were available. Furthermore, uncertainty surrounded not only the government's financial measures and the rules which it imposed to limit responses, but also the extent of the losses which might be suffered. For instance, it might be possible to ignore the rules, to challenge the validity of government measures and to opt for a 'rebel-lious' stance (increase expenditure and increase rates), as some authorities did, but the consequences of such action in the short, medium and long term could not easily be pre-dicted.

As time went on, the negative effects became cumulative, and there was not the opportunity, as with the more acute form of crisis analysed by Jackson (1976), and Billings, Milburn and Schaalman (1980), to return to the status quo or somewhere near it. The crisis was extended and intermittent rather than singular and acute.

Even in these circumstances the question of time is important, for with financial, as distinct from physical, crises, there is a normal cycle of events which is built into the system. This is an annual flow of figures representing estimates by spending units, assessments by controlling and validating committees, reformulations by spending units and further validation by senior officers, councillors and, finally, the council. It is upon these figures that the whole of the activities of the authority are based, plans are made, contracts are entered into and projects started and maintained.

The cycle exists not simply to satisfy budgetary requirements but to facilitate the particular form of policy-making found in most local authorities. There must be time for plans to be examined, dissent to be heard, alternatives to be put forward and for debate and open discussion. The authority has to be seen to be accountable to the community it serves, and this means involving councillors, officers and, wherever possible, other interested parties in the process. All of this takes time and has to be carefully planned.

The uncertainty surrounding the government's intentions and future actions, and the short time-scale with which they were announced or changed, caused considerable confusion in local authority committees responsible for maintaining the cycle of events. The situation can be likened to placing an obstruction between the spokes of a moving bicycle wheel, withdrawing it and replacing it again intermittently and with no warning.

The crisis, therefore, provided three major problems: cumulative negative effects upon certain services, the outcomes of which became more and more obvious as time passed; less and less room for manoeuvre in order to find solutions; and disruption of time-honoured and much valued organizational, professional and political procedures of decision-making. Steps taken to cope with these problems led to the establishment of a crisis culture.

The control of singular crises normally calls for extraordinary measures which in other circumstances would not be tolerated. As the crisis subsides there should be a return to near normality as the special measures are no longer required. In the extended-intermittent crisis, however, there is no return to the previously existing situation, and the special circumstances which emerge to cope with the crisis remain over a relatively long period of time.

Uncertainty is at the heart of the culture. This is likely to be manifested in three ways: defensiveness, a shift in the locus of key decision-making, and lowered morale. These elements of the crisis culture are dealt with in turn.

Defensiveness

Defensiveness is a natural corollary of uncertainty. It implies a cautious attitude towards new ventures, a lowered positive responsiveness to overtures from others and less willingness to co-operate. Attitudes become introverted and the main concern becomes protection of one's own interests – individual or departmental.

Defensive strategies have been noted by several writers concerned with organizations. Simon, Smithberg and Thompson (1950) describe tactics largely concerned with seeking outside support, strengthening old alliances and forging new ones. Levine (1978) talks of 'retrenchment politics' which lead to 'scepticism, cynicism, distrust and non-compliance'.

Greenwood (1983) describes tactics sometimes employed by chief officers in local authorities to gain support and to head off cuts:

> Sometimes information about reductions being considered would be made available to a wider public and would contain items of expenditure known to be politically sensitive . . . One director of education made public the number of teaching posts that might have to be discontinued, along with the names of several village schools that would have to be closed.
>
> (p. 157)

This strategy is what Greenwood calls 'waving the bloody stump or shroud waving'. But if, as is often the case, each department seeks to defend its own interests and uncompromisingly to resist cuts, there is an increasing chance of conflict. Cyert (1978), considering the case of universities in a contracting situation, indicates the problems likely to arise:

> Conflict resolution will be more difficult in a contracting organization because the easy method of utilizing more resources for resolution is not available . . . The added dimension of participants competing with each other for a limited number of positions and sub-units competing with each other for a limited number of organizational slots clearly increases the tension level in the organization.
>
> (p. 348)

This is a statement which could also apply to most local authorities coping with a crisis culture.

Jackson (1976) also points to the limited nature of the responses available in a crisis and to the absence of longer-term considerations. The basic mode of decision-making, he maintains, is incrementalist and this adds to defensiveness:

> Short run considerations will be paramount, not long range planning. The search for solutions in the impact stage will be in the realm of solutions which have been employed in the past. Partial solutions are likely because the usual response to a crisis will be the least possible change to return to the status quo.
>
> (p. 223)

Pettigrew (1983) notes a similar response:

> Faced with gathering environmental pressure, and possibly conflict and confusion about the extent of the difficulties and how to respond to them, 'do as before but more' may be the response. High levels of uncertainty and its handmaiden, high fear of failure, in a system with strong needs for achievement, can produce the implementation of safe action programmes which may not be well tuned to new environmental circumstances and needs.
>
> (p. 107)

Levine (1978) suggests a similar pattern in declining public sector institutions. He argues that, in the face of cut-back, managers will choose the least risky course and attempt to protect organizational capacity and procedures by trying to 'smooth' decline and its effects upon the organization.

The short-run considerations of the crisis culture make it similar in this respect to the *laissez-faire* culture discussed earlier. In *laissez-faire* there was no great motivation to evaluate existing practices nor to consider a range of alternatives for future action. In crisis there is not the time – or so it seems. But as the crisis lengthens and persists there emerges what Stewart (1977) refers to as 'the certainty of uncertainty'. The recurrence of the crisis eventually becomes almost predictable, and, in theory at least, it should be possible to plan in advance by devising a series of alternative responses to meet new situations as they arise. This, as will be seen in Part III of this book, could lead from a crisis to a cuts culture.

The Locus of Decision-Making

Uncertainty, defensiveness and lowered morale are significant indicators of the crisis culture. They are often linked to a change in the leadership style of the institution, indicating a shift in the balance of power.

A crisis, if it is to be survived, demands resolute action. Normal procedures may not be adequate for this task and may have to be overridden or circumscribed. How this is done and who does it depends upon both the nature of the crisis and the nature of the organization. In extreme circumstances, as in some of the national emergencies studied by Jackson (1976), force will be used. This is not likely to occur in local government organizations, but the circumstances which lead up to the situation may be similar. The need for resolute action in the face of uncertainty and confusion causes a shift in the locus of power. Those who seem able to cope with the situation and find acceptable solutions will be accorded the power to take action, and this power may go beyond that to which they are normally accustomed.

Hickson *et al.* (1973) argue that power will be accorded to those organizational units which are best able to cope with uncertainty and in so doing help the organization to survive. They maintain that the more central their decisions and actions are for the organization, and the less it is possible to find effective substitutes for the individuals or departments who are able to cope, the more power they will be accorded. Jackson (1976) points out that in a national crisis, 'the normal intermediary groups of a liberal society rarely have much role to play'. Crises thus tend to lead towards the centralization of power and autocratic styles of leadership, a point confirmed by Glassberg (1978).

What is produced is, in effect, an accelerated form of Michels's 'iron law of oligarchy' which holds that the larger and more complex the organization the more it is likely that power will ultimately come to reside in the hands of a small élite group who control the key processes (Michels, 1962). In Michels's argument, contenders connive and deviously manipulate the system in order to achieve the power they seek. In a crisis such tactics are unnecessary since the complexities facing the organization become so great that power is simply accorded to those who can best cope. Either way the 'iron law' seems to operate.

Greenwood (1983) studied several local authorities and the procedures which they followed during a period of severe financial constraint. He likens the situation to a form of 'Spanish Inquisition' which relies upon private meetings of the powerful figures outside of the committee system. This sums up the shift of power experienced by many authorities in the crisis culture.

The Social Climate – Morale
Because of uncertainty, defensiveness and, in education, the identity crisis referred to earlier, there is almost certain to be a problem of morale. The pleasures of building are replaced by the problems of dismantling, and the process may be accompanied by the fear of job loss. Easy working relationships established during a period of growth may come under

strain as loyalty to one group rather than another is demanded. There are likely to be increased pressures as more work is expected with less resources. But worst of all for the committed professional is the sense of failure surrounding ideals that have been worked for over a career and which are now questioned and possibly discredited.

Stewart (1977), referring to local authorities, has little doubt as to the severity of the problem:

> It is the staff who bear the costs. It is the staff who have lost the clear goals that were based on growth. There was a real sense of achievement that came from the massive capital programmes and from the improvement of services. Staff who have lost the sense of purpose given by growth now have to find a new sense of purpose. It is not easy when the predominant voice heard is that of press or public criticism. The real crisis of local government is a crisis of morale and the first task is to recognise this.
>
> (p. 20)

Alongside the feelings of frustration and failure go pressures to change, to innovate and to economize. A study of stress in one educational institution (Castling, 1983) indicates the extent of the pressures on staff. The study revealed thirty-three significant changes which had affected most staff over a five-year period. Many of these changes required the rapid building of new relationships and the learning of new skills and ways of doing things; these caused disturbance, stress and lowered morale. Caldicott (1985) examining organizational causes of stress on teachers notes the importance of 'an over-competitive atmosphere, unclear job requirements, lack of recognition and inadequate credit'.

These aspects of a crisis culture – uncertainty, defensiveness, shift in the locus of power and lowered morale – will now be examined in relation to Shire and to the management of the educational service within the county.

Shire and Uncertainty

In Chapter 6 the cuts imposed upon the service were analysed. Apart from the reductions associated with falling rolls, the main areas of saving identified were the physical environment, teaching support services including ancillary staff, and special activities such as swimming, music and environmental studies. There was also the controversial reduction of one hundred teachers following the annual pay settlement in 1981. Cuts over the period under review amounted to more than £6 million.

The need for these cuts is now examined. Why was education, amongst the other services, singled out to make such substantial savings? Why did the education committee choose to make cuts in these particular areas? And finally, under what circumstances were the cuts made?

To answer these questions it is necessary to see the education service in Shire as an integral part of a local authority and, despite a certain degree of independence, still subject to the overall control of the council.

Uncertainty on All Sides

The starting point for the annual cycle of financial planning in local authorities is the government's statement of intent for the following financial year set out in the White Paper on public expenditure. This reaches local authorities about February and indicates to them, on a service-by-service basis, expenditure plans for the following year, leaving about fourteen months before the start of the financial year to which the White Paper applies.

A major innovation in 1977 was the introduction of cash limits. The government specified what it was prepared to pay for services rather than what it was prepared to buy. Increases in prices would, therefore, generally have the effect of reducing the volume of services. In setting targets the government took into account the current year's expenditure, adjusted this for policy changes and added an amount, e.g. 4 per cent, to allow for price increases. To exceed set targets was to risk a penalty in the form of a reduced grant. This procedure, subject to various additional controls and sanctions, has remained in force to the present time.

In Shire it falls to the County Treasurer to interpret the implications of the White Paper for officers and members. His report is normally made available to chief officers and committee chairmen* in March or April. Following meetings between officers and chairmen, a paper setting out implications and options is submitted to the policy and resources committee in June. After approval the various service committees are asked to review their priorities for the coming year on the basis of the new guidelines.

Between October and December the budgets are prepared by each department ready for the announcement of the government's rate support grant figures in late December. Following this, the budget for the forthcoming year is approved by the policy and resources committee, the new rate is fixed and the process ends with final approval by the council in February. At least this is what happens in relatively 'normal' times.

The problem is that for nearly a decade White Papers have specified a slowing down or a reduction in local authority spending. Thus the budgetary process starts off each year with a demand to save money. The early meetings, involving the County Treasurer, Chief Executive, Chairman of Council and chairmen of the various spending committees, are concerned with determining where savings can be made. It should be repeated here that Shire Council made, and has adhered to, a policy of not incurring penalties by exceeding government targets.

The White Paper is concerned with overall public expenditure for each service. It does not specify spending for each separate authority at this time. Eventually each council receives a block grant over which, in theory at least, it retains the right to allocate the money according to its own local needs. The block grant is, however, based upon calculations for each service, for each individual authority, which are

---

* During the period under review all those occupying this role were men.

made by the government according to grant-related expenditure formulae (GREs). The time of publication of these detailed GREs has an important bearing on the financial manoeuvrings which take place within councils. Travers (1983) explains the position as follows:

> In fact GREs for each service are not published along with the rest of the statistical paraphernalia of block grant before Christmas. While the Department of Education and Science would be happy to release them then, the local authorities object to service by service GRE's being made available before budgets are set. The authorities argue that ratepayer and pressure groups would ask why proposed spending deviated from GRE for the service, and thus put pressure on councillors to spend up or down.
>
> (p. 332)

The position at the beginning of a financial cycle, then, is that the County Treasurer and Chief Executive, using the White Paper for the coming year, discuss with the chief officers of the spending units and the chairmen of their associated committees how the council can keep within government targets. The result of these discussions is a request to all departments (or more recently to specific departments, especially education) to determine how they might reduce their expected budget by x per cent for the coming year.

The process involved in reaching decisions on the allocation of these savings between departments, and the subsequent difficulties arising at the committee and implementation stages, is fraught with problems and uncertainty.

The interpretation of the White Paper is no more than a best estimate of what the government will do as regards local authority financing in the next fourteen months. The language used in the White Paper and subsequent supporting statements is complicated; there are inevitable ambiguities; new rules are added and old ones changed from year to year, and the actual rate support grant is not made known until very late on in the budgetary cycle.

The rate of inflation and, usually associated with it, the trend in local government wage settlements (not least for teachers) are difficult to predict exactly. Both might exceed the centrally determined cash limits, thus imposing the need for further cost-cutting exercises (as was illustrated by Shire's decision to reduce the teaching force by one hundred after the 1981 pay settlement).

The following extracts from a statement made by the treasurer to the policy and resources committee in January 1982 indicate the difficulties involved in 'getting it right' in any one year. (NB 'Shire' has been substituted for the actual name of the County.)

Before dealing with the question of 1982/83 and recommending a rate it is important to look at the latest estimate for the current year 1981/82. On this occasion I have included a re-run of the trials and tribulations of the year, particularly as many Councillors were not present until May.

December, 1980
Deficit of £2.4 million forecast for the 31 March, 1981. Urgent steps taken by all departments to stop spending.

January/February, 1981
The Council levied a rate of 120 pence which included 3.86 pence for the estimated overspending in 1980/81 of £2.4 million. Grant position very vague. Council's spending target announced by the Department of the Environment after the budget meeting.

2nd June, Secretary of State indicated that Shire would suffer a £3 million grant penalty on its original 1981/82 budget. Revised budgets requested.

Final accounts for 1980/81 showed that the £2.4 million overspending had been reduced to £107,000 by the efforts of everyone. Therefore, £2.3 million flowed into balances . . .

October, 1981
. . . Notified of decision taken by Secretary of State to allow grant related expenditure to be substituted for the expendi-

ture target based on 1978/79 levels where this was more favourable.

After considerable discussion with the Department of the Environment concerning the treatment of revenue bills, and after suspending repayments to the reserve fund, Shire was declared to be £4,000 below its grant related expenditure.

(Grant related expenditure was referred to in my report of the 14th October, 1981, as a 'movable feast'.)

December, 1981
The 'movable feast' moved. The Department of the Environment increased grant related expenditure by £1.6 million on adjustments which could not possibly have been predicted . . .

The result of all this activity and changing financial parameters means that it is now estimated that there will be £6.323 million in balances at 31st March, 1982 . . .

The above quotations, which are part of a much longer report, serve to indicate just how complicated the system has become and how uncertain the financial position of the council can be at any one time. Shire's situation vacillated considerably over the course of the year in question, beginning with an apparent deficit of over £2 million and ending with what seemed to be a surplus of about £6 million. Needless to say that surplus evaporated within the ensuing six months to become an equally large deficit, which had to be covered by further savings.

The treasurer mentioned, at the beginning of his report, councillors who 'were not present until May'. This was a reference to the newly elected council of 1981 which brought in a high proportion of first-time members. Relevant at this point, however, is the apparent need to explain the situation to those people who had recently acquired membership of, and were trying to orientate themselves within, a rapidly changing organizational environment.

The difficulty of coming to terms with so much complex financial language and so many new concepts and rules was a major task for many councillors who possessed only a limited knowledge of accounting and of the central–local government principles which underpinned the whole procedure. Several councillors raised this point during interviews. They felt 'out on a limb' when it came to a discussion of financial matters. Two examples will illustrate the difficult task they faced in trying to sort out not only the language but also the 'pecuniary chess games' played out under its mantle.

One councillor admitted finding the concept of grant-related expenditure difficult to understand. On looking it up in a Department of the Environment explanatory booklet (DOE, 1980) he found the following:

> Under the new block grant system an authority's grant entitlement is calculated from its total expenditure in the following way. For any given level of expenditure by the authority in relation to need the Rate Support Grant Report lays down a notional rate poundage – the 'grant related poundage' – which for the purposes of the grant calculation they are assumed to levy towards that level of expenditure. There is a common tariff which determines the amount by which an individual authority's assumed rate poundage will change as it chooses to increase or decrease its level of expenditure.
>
> (p. 1)

Perhaps the idea could have been explained more simply, but as it stands the reader, in order to understand it fully, must have some knowledge of other concepts such as 'block grant system', 'notional rate poundage', 'grant related poundage' and 'common tariff'. And if the block grant system is to be understood well enough to allow the councillor to engage in serious arguments with the 'financial experts' he might feel it necessary to refer to an explanatory article on the subject in *Local Government Studies* (Gibson, 1982). There he will find the following:

> The basic structure of the block grant thus incorporated two changes which could help to reduce local authority expenditure. Firstly, there was the taper on the rate of grant support given to any local authority spending above the threshold.

Secondly, there was via the common GRP function the introduction of negative marginal rates of grant for those authorities whose GRV exceeded the (implicit) NSRV.

(p. 20)

For many councillors the effort of coming to terms with a whole new language built upon complex principles of financial control is too much to expect. This effectively excludes them from active participation in many issues that are crucial to local government policy-making.

But not all councillors fall into this category. Some do have considerable financial knowledge and are prepared to use it. The results, however, are not always as they expect, as the following incident illustrates.

A newly elected Labour councillor whose Civil Service job required him to have knowledge of statistics and accounting earned a reputation as a 'figures man'. He was appointed to the falling rolls working party and realized that it was a 'vast statistical exercise' which few members really understood. He acted as spokesman for the group made up of all political parties. He noticed then the manner in which 'officers influenced the members by presenting figures in a particular way'.

He began to take a particular interest in financial statements and found one set of figures relating to school meals which he did not understand, nor could he get a satisfactory explanation from officers. There seemed to be a discrepancy of about £100,000. After some research he decided to raise the matter in the education committee, and this caused the matter to be referred back to a subcommittee for further investigation.

What he had uncovered turned out to be a legitimate accounting procedure but one which had been used in a particular way to help the education committee show a 'book' saving necessary to meet its target in that particular accounting period. As he realized later he had caused considerable difficulties for officers and even greater cuts for a service he was concerned to protect because some money had to be returned to a central fund. Had he been 'in the know' he would have supported the presentation of the figures in their original form.

Uncertainty underlies and pervades the cuts culture. As was suggested earlier, it is generally accompanied by other factors – defensiveness, a shift in the locus of power, and a change in the social climate affecting morale. These are considered next as they influenced the culture in Shire and the education service in particular.

Defensiveness

There were two areas in which defensiveness emerged in the crisis culture: through the political system and through the departmental system. By the mid-1970s, later than in many other authorities, Shire was beginning to see the growth of hard-edged political ideologies at the expense of the previously much valued localism.

There were a number of reasons for this. It reflected the position nationally where consensus between the parties on any major issue was the exception rather than the rule. It was influenced by the increasing politicization of the local authority associations including the Association of County Councils; it was affected by the integration of 'the City' (previously a county borough) and its grammar schools into the new county council following local government reorganization in 1974; it reflected 'the new wave of conservatism' and the different styles and attitudes of councillors (often middle class, small business owners) elected to the council in the 1977 elections; and finally, but not until 1981, it was a manifestation of a relatively new phenomenon: a large minority made up of Labour and Liberal members.

All of these factors together meant that the easy-going, club-like atmosphere of the 1960s was a thing of the past. The new Conservatives were concerned with making savings to avoid increases in the rates; with law and order and with educational 'standards and accountability' in the service. The new Labour group, in accordance with its own party's national campaign, was determined to resist all cuts. Conflict was inevitable and the new aggressive attitudes were immediately apparent at committee meetings, as all proposals for savings were objected to and counter-proposals were put forward for restoring earlier cuts.

All the parties blamed each other for the deep divisions and incessant wrangling which surrounded policy debates. Outsiders, such as added members on the education committee (who are co-opted and not elected), admitted to being 'appalled at the low level of discussion brought about by the desire to score political points'.

Political defensiveness, then, became a feature of the crisis culture in Shire, but there is one important qualification. The senior party members and committee chairmen were, by and large, not from the new Conservative group. They still carried with them many of the more traditional attitudes and values and they were often as keen as senior officers to defend services they had helped to build. They did not take kindly to cuts nor to central government interference as they saw it. Some of the strongest criticisms of government policy, or lack of it, came from leading Conservative councillors who, as a result, were sometimes branded 'wets' by their more politically aggressive colleagues.

In education, successive chairmen have committed themselves to 'their service' and have shown strong attachment to earlier policies, particularly comprehensive reorganization, despite growing resistance from other party members and disapproval of new schemes by the Secretary of State.

Defensiveness also manifested itself in departmental strategies to avoid cuts. One of the first casualties of this was the corporate management system which had begun to emerge during the period of planned growth. The principles underlying this approach to organizational management – including, for instance, inter-departmental collaboration, needs analysis, specification of goals and objectives, cost-benefit analysis applied to alternative courses of action, monitoring and evaluation of performance – all require careful forward planning, identification of corporate, as distinct from departmental, goals and time to assess alternative solutions to emerging problems. The crisis culture, full of uncertainty, based upon contraction rather than growth and posing problems to be solved within short time-limits, runs counter to the normal requirements of corporatism.

The innovative, and still experimental, 'programme budgeting system' was soon abandoned – although, according to a few committed officers, some of its concepts and procedures remained as an influence on policy-making.

The corporate approach itself, embodying team meetings at departmental head and deputy head level, inter-departmental planning groups, joint working parties, etc., continued to produce a flow of reports and recommendations. But, overall, the effects upon crisis policy-making were limited, and there was both ignorance about the system and cynicism about its usefulness amongst councillors and senior and junior staff, some of whom were members of corporate teams.

Corporatism and defensiveness are by their nature not compatible, and in the crisis culture there may be good reason why people act defensively. Consider, for instance, the problems of a head of department who is also a member of a corporate team which has the unenviable task of finding savings of, say £2 million for the fifth year in succession. Perhaps for the first two or three years he would be prepared to acquiesce with the 'fair shares for all' procedure in which each department accepts a similar percentage cut. But this is hardly corporate management, and the senior officer will eventually find that the approach shifts towards what Greenwood (1983) calls 'option percentage planning' – each department having to identify reductions in service provision of varying degrees of severity, e.g. 2, 3, or 5 per cent. The intention behind this approach is, as Greenwood explains, 'to discriminate between services in the incidence of cuts and a recognized need to compose lists of possible cuts that would allow reallocation of resources between services' (p. 153). However committed to corporate management the head of department is, he is bound to have considerable problems in accepting such a proposition due to his expected loyalty to his department.

Further cuts may well entail job losses, and wherever the

axe falls it will be painful and probably involve confrontation with the unions. At some point, and while still maintaining a corporate front, the chief has to devise strategies for defending the service for which he is responsible.

In these circumstances all services seem bound to make the best case possible to defend themselves from cuts; and in Shire, as elsewhere, some services were eventually to be preserved at the expense of others. Police and fire services, for instance, were largely protected by government regulations, and indeed some modest growth was stipulated for police and magistrates' courts. The government was also urging more capital expenditure on roads and buildings, and this, through higher debt charges, was bound to increase revenue costs for some departments. The library service was always popular with the public, and cuts in this area were regarded as politically very difficult.

A major spender, the social services department, was at the start of the crisis period, by comparison with many other local authorities, less well financed. Its case for more rather than less funds was a strong one; particularly with rising unemployment and a proportion of old people steadily exceeding the national average. Other small services had already been severely cut, and to reduce them still further would threaten their viability. Finally, central administration had, over several years, taken its share of the cuts and was itself under increasing pressure due to extra work generated by the need to find and implement savings.

Where, then, could extra savings be found in these circumstances? They would hardly be volunteered by departmental heads in true altruistic corporate fashion! But they had to be found somewhere given the council's commitment to a policy of 'no penalties'. Attention inevitably focussed on education.

Defending Education　As the demands by government and the council increased year by year the pressure on senior officers and education committee members to ensure that standards were not affected also increased. Pressure groups inside and outside of the council chamber became more active. Politicians, parents, teachers, other school staff, professional associations and unions, community groups and in some cases representatives of the churches, local industry and commerce added their weight to the policy debate. The unpredictability of these otherwise latent pressures added a further dimension to the uncertainty underlying the crisis culture. How did education cope in these circumstances? How did it defend itself and how did it attempt to limit the negative effects of the cuts?

One way relates to what was referred to in the last section as 'shroud waving'. The Chief Education Officer, as well as spelling out the effects of the cuts, would often remind councillors of the fact that the county was spending less than other authorities and would quote the relevant statistical league tables to prove the point. He would also point out that the service was facing a number of increased commitments, thus making it extremely difficult to find further savings.

In the resource plan for 1983/4 he stressed the fact that there were eight important areas where growth rather than contraction was necessary. Some of these seemed unavoidable, e.g. additional educational psychologists to meet the terms of the 1981 Education Act, or more careers advisers necessary in a time of high youth unemployment. Other areas such as the restoration of some welfare assistance in primary schools were known to be politically popular with councillors and the public.

At the end of a carefully worded statement pulling together the effects of further cuts, the already lowly place of the county in the league tables for the whole country and the need for more expenditure to meet pressing commitments, he added: 'The committee is therefore asked to define how it wishes to respond to the County Council's call to illustrate savings of £2,150,000 plus a further £140,000 to cover the increased manual worker costs'. Put in this way the statement places heavy responsibility for demanding further cuts on the council and was bound to raise feelings which might steer members towards preserving the status quo.

But there was also a major factor which permeated the whole policy debate, colouring it, confusing it and above all making education the focal point of the cuts in the county, and at the same time making savings possible. This was the 1970s and 1980s problem of falling rolls. As Walsh *et al.* (1982) note:

> Local government expenditure has been falling in real terms for some years. From 1973/4 to 1980/81 local government capital and current expenditure fell by 16.6% ... The climate of educational planning – particularly in shire counties – has been one of limited resources together with falling rolls. Teasing out the interactions between these phenomena is virtually impossible and probably fruitless in any event.
>
> (p. 12)

Teasing out the interaction may indeed be fruitless as an academic exercise, but in terms of resource allocation in an authority experiencing severe financial constraint it becomes a central issue.

Falling rolls are an unusual, and it would seem temporary, phenomenon in education and one that has been much studied by educators, administrators, statisticians and accountants alike – see Manning *et al.* (1982) for a comprehensive annotated bibliography. It is, as the councillor quoted earlier suggested, 'a vast statistical exercise which few members really understood'; but it is also clear from the literature and from the actions taken by some authorities that the statistics mask a range of potentially creative decisions.

It was generally accepted in Shire that falling rolls created structural problems due to the uneven nature of the decline which could not easily be handled by the normal pupil–teacher ratio method of staffing. It was agreed to study alternative approaches which might help to cushion the effects. Because of this a working group was set up in 1979 and 'curriculum-led staffing' was one such approach considered. Curriculum-led staffing is described by Walsh *et al.* (1982) as follows:

The aim is to make it possible to vary assumptions about curriculum policy. The amount of teaching time needed in a school depends upon the number of classes formed, which in turn depends upon what is to be taught, for what length of time, to what proportion of pupils, in what combination and in what sizes of teaching groups. Account is also taken in this approach of non-teaching time, and the approach is then used to calculate overall teacher demand.

(p. 49)

This sums up the approach adopted by the working group in Shire. It expressed the aims of the new model as follows: 'to maintain the curriculum during the years of decline; provide adaptability and flexibility in staffing and allow plans to be made several years ahead to meet changing demands on the service'.

A policy decision was eventually made by the education committee to protect staffing ratios and the curriculum in secondary schools against the effects of the decline in the school population. This decision led to the creation of a 'curriculum model' for the county. As a result of the new formula for calculating staffing, most schools received a slightly better establishment than before. This helped to provide a cushion for the difficulties which lay ahead.

The curriculum model was drawn up by officers but was carefully worked out in detail with heads and unions and was painstakingly explained to councillors as the following extract from the working group's report shows:

During the course of the development work a general paper had been put to Committee which gave a broad outline of the problem, but at the conclusion of the work it was felt necessary to organise a seminar for members of the Education Staffing Sub-Committee and Personal Services Sub-Committee. The detail of the falling rolls problem in Shire was explained and the opportunity taken to demonstrate that pro-rata reduction in teaching staffs was inappropriate.

The last point was an important one to establish. As a result of the considerable efforts made to explain and 'sell' the model, it received general acclaim as a major and valuable innovation in helping secondary schools to meet the falling rolls problem.

It was not seen as a necessarily defensive measure at the time; rather it was regarded as a sensible form of planning. After the scheme was implemented, however, it proved a useful policy plank in the crisis culture and, although complicated in detail, it had about it the aura of a strong positive defence against unnecessary erosion of the curriculum.

It was, in retrospect, described by the Chief Education Officer as a 'valuable psychological symbol and a rallying point' for most councillors whatever their political persuasion. Despite the fact that each year after its implementation the education committee was expected to find savings, usually in the region of £1 to £2 million, the staffing establishment associated with the curriculum model was eroded only once and then by a relatively small amount. Furthermore, moves were subsequently made at a number of committee meetings to reinstate the loss which remained as a thorn in the flesh of those who had so strongly supported the model in the first place.

There were other respects in which falling rolls became the focus of cost-saving battles. Because falls are not even across areas and across schools, because they do not respect pupil–teacher ratios and normal class sizes, because not all schools are the same size, because not all teachers (bearing in mind age, experience and specialism) are equally dispensable, and because savings on overheads brought about by closing a part of a school are not proportionate to the total overheads, there is no direct and easily calculated relationship between a numerical fall in pupil numbers and the financial saving that can be obtained therefrom.

The complexity of the statistical, financial exercise and the various arguments that can be used for presenting figures in one way rather than another ensure that the savings obtainable from falling rolls are never cut and dried. Consequently they are not easily understood by those outside of the education department.

Falling rolls is, therefore, a situation that can be used to produce savings to satisfy the demands of a cuts-hungry government but, at the same time, can also be used to protect the service from some of the worst effects of continual cutting. It allows some flexibility and breathing space in the downward spiral of expenditure.

The primary sector, which was the first to feel the effects of falling rolls, and was not covered by the curriculum model, also had to be defended. As shown in Chapter 6, the cost per pupil in a small school is much higher than in a larger one, and falling rolls meant even more smaller schools. Those seeking savings, therefore, looked hard at the possibility of wholesale closure of small schools, and it was at one time advocated by hard-line councillors that any school with less than sixty pupils should be closed. This would have meant closing down over a quarter of the primary schools in the county and would have caused considerable community reaction and the loss of many teaching posts, which would certainly have been strongly opposed by the unions.

The Chief Education Officer admits that it was a difficult task persuading members to accept a policy of closure only when numbers fell below thirty. But once achieved this meant a much slower rate of closure and a reduction in teaching numbers that could be managed largely by an early-retirement scheme. The pupil–teacher ratio was preserved and the social cost of closing village schools was minimized.

So what emerged as a basic policy guideline for both primary and secondary schools in the crisis culture was the protection of staffing ratios associated with the maintenance of curriculum standards. This was the defence adopted by education and one which those outside found it hard to penetrate. But under pressure from the council, itself under pressure from the government, some savings had to be made and these had to be found elsewhere. It was, therefore, necessary to order priorities and to defend certain elements of the service at the expense of others.

Education is not a homogeneous service. It is a diverse collection of inputs ranging from classroom teaching to the provision of meals and transport. The policy issue revolves upon the questions, Which of these inputs can reasonably be reduced and by what amount in order to cause least harm?

What was suggested by the Chief Education Officer and Chairman of Education and eventually, reluctantly, accepted by most of the committee was a banding system in which the various inputs were classified as 'protected, semi-protected and potentially cutable'. This system was later extended to a staged model as follows:

Stage 1: reducing or abandoning non-essential provision, e.g. conference centres,
Stage 2: paring down levels of expenditure in any area,
Stage 3: reducing or abandoning indirect educational support, e.g. road crossing patrols, clothing allowances,
Stage 4: reducing direct educational support, e.g. welfare assistance and school meals,
Stage 5: reducing direct educational provision, e.g. the teaching force, books and materials.

Although, in practice, this model provided only a tentative framework rather than a strict procedural device it did have the effect of indicating to members in which area of generally agreed priorities proposed cuts were likely to fall.

Associated with this form of priority setting was a further system of negative options. This comprised a listing of possible cuts indicating the actions which could be taken, the likely consequences of such actions and the financial and staffing savings which would accrue. The statement would normally go first to the finance subcommittee for consideration and then to the education committee. The following extracts from the 1982/3 statement illustrate the flavour:

Nursery/Welfare assistance. Abolish. Saving £280,000. Would undermine education standards in infant years – leaving teachers with no classroom support . . . FTE Staff Reduction 71.4.

Secretarial assistance. Reduce by one third in primary, secondary and special schools. Savings £130,000, £207,000, £19,500. Would leave schools without telephone cover or adequate support staff in day-to-day organisation, communication with parents, health and support services, industry and employers for example. FTE Staff Reduction 34, 39 and 4.

Clothing grants. Abolish. Saving £29,600. Would leave children of poorer families unable to provide school uniform requirements.

School leaver courses. Abolish. Saving £29,000. Withdrawal of L.E.A. from responsibility to assist transition to adult world and to work. FTE Staff Reduction 2.

In the statement from which these extracts are taken, options are suggested for savings totalling £4.7 million. Decisions as to where to cut are not easily made, but at least the various options are spelled out and members can discuss the possibilities on the basis of a previously agreed set of priorities.

Thus, there is a form of policy based upon the notion of expendability for certain items set against core protected areas. Apart from the one much disputed saving of a hundred teachers related to the curriculum model, the cuts have taken place mainly in areas of indirect provision leaving stage 5 above more or less untouched.

The cuts that were made eventually were not random and they were guided by a certain logic based upon the assessment of priorities. But were the decisions still based on short-term options and might other decisions, based upon longer-term considerations, have produced less negative outcomes?

The second question is impossible to answer although some speculations are made in Part III of the book. The first question, however, has to be answered in the affirmative. By and large what was cut was what could be cut. The savings became progressively harder to find as the cuts worked their way from the periphery to the centre of the teaching enterprise – the classroom. In one sense this was the most logical procedure but it left major questions about the nature, goals and structure of the service unexamined. The inevitable outcome was that the service would, as far as possible, continue as it was but become relatively under-resourced in certain areas.

A Shift in the Locus of Power
There are a number of consequences which arise from uncertainty and defensiveness as previously discussed:

(1) Many members feel left out of the real process of decision-making.
(2) They feel obliged to leave major decisions on financial matters to 'those who know the ropes'.
(3) Those who are really in the know and are able to 'play the government at their own game' are accorded considerable power. This certainly includes the County Treasurer and the Chief Executive.
(4) Because many decisions are urgent, the power of those who are able to cope well on behalf of the council in conditions of crisis is further enhanced.

Because it became so difficult for departments to impose cuts upon themselves, and because departments were forced to take an increasingly defensive stance as the crisis continued, decisions relating to contraction had to be taken elsewhere. The normal mechanisms built into the corporate approach became increasingly difficult to use. Senior officers were becoming adept at presenting strong cases for the preservation of their own department and also reasons why others should bear the brunt of the cuts.

Eventually senior councillors were forced to play a more directive role – a role which some officers felt they should have taken many years earlier.

In 1982 for the first time the Chairman of Council met with the chairmen of service committees, in private, without any officers present. The outcome of this meeting was an allocation of resources for the following year in which social services and police were protected and other services, including education, took a larger share of the cuts. This represented a major shift in the locus of policy-making.

Furthermore, at a time when financial strategies dominated policy-making in local government it is difficult to identify a more important department than that of the County Treasurer. The more this department was able to produce solutions to deal with the pressing crises the more influential became its senior officers.

But a treasurer has the power to advise and influence policy, not to make or implement it. Here the administrative power of the Chief Executive and the political power of the Council Chairman are important. This triumvirate may be regarded as an élite group wielding considerably more power than they might normally expect or even wish for. It was nevertheless towards this group that the locus of power eventually shifted in Shire.

Greenwood (1983) might have been referring to Shire when he described the process of budgetary allocation in the several authorities he studied:

> Thus, when the initial departmental bids have been received by the treasurer a series of meetings takes place between central politician(s) and officers. Often these meetings will involve only the leader, the treasurer and the chief executive . . . These actors are linked to wider parts of the authority by virtue of other significant groups. The treasurer and chief executive will meet colleagues on their management team, when expressions of concern will come from service chief officers. The leader tries to balance the pressures for restraining with those for spending, he has to satisfy himself that the party will support budgetary proposals once they emerge in the formal committee system. Essentially these private meetings and consultations take place early in the formative stages of the resource allocation process. Much political mobilisation occurs at this point although none of it happens at committee.
>
> A second series of private meetings occurs later in the process. These meetings were described by one authority leader as the 'sweat shop'. At these, the leader, chief executive and the treasurer meet with the chairman and chief officer of each service in turn. The service is notified of the amount of

spending that can be supported, and the volume of service
reductions required. Counter proposals may be made. The
outcome is that each chief officer takes back his share of
resources to his department and begins the revision of
estimates. The privacy of these meetings should not be
underestimated.

(p. 163)

Finally there is a shift in party political power. As the
rank-and-file members are left out of the major decision-
making processes, and as the main political parties cease to
co-operate, the influential figures in the majority party come
more to the fore. Jennings (1977) neatly sums up the position
as it applied to Shire:

Clearly, increased party political control of local councils
tends to mean an increased centralization of decision-making
in policy matters, a decrease in the control and administration of services by committees and a shift in emphasis of
committee chairmen's roles from service representatives to
political advisors.

(p. 67)

To sum up the situation in Shire, there was a definite shift in
the locus of major decision-making to a small group who
were able to make the unpopular decisions relating to the
cuts and enforce their implementation through their own
power networks. This situation accords with the thesis put
forward by Hickson *et al.* (1973) that power will be accorded
to those units within the organization most able to ensure
survival during a time of uncertainty. But as a result other
units become relatively less powerful and therefore more
submissive to the requirements of the new central power
élite. There is little doubt that the education service in Shire
found itself in this 'underdog' position and that it was forced
to make savings on a scale which those within the service
deemed harmful. As will be seen in the following chapters
this situation has continued into 1985.

The Social Climate

The continuance of the many factors associated with the cuts culture eventually produced a change in the social climate. The competitive edge brought about as a result of the struggle to obtain resources and to 'balance the books' produced obvious strains in previously good relationships both within and outside of the department.

Those with major responsibilities for policy-making found themselves under pressure from all sides; in the long term they could please nobody, and theirs was a 'no win' situation. They were engaged in a process of dismantling a service they had originally helped to build, and the individual and social problems which this caused were often painful in themselves, quite apart from the need to undertake actions considered to be detrimental educationally.

In education there sometimes seemed to be a siege situation. Everyone outside of the department appeared to be against the service. Staff reductions centrally meant fewer administrators to carry out the difficult and sensitive tasks associated with contraction. Praise was rare. Criticism was frequent. Transposition from the role of concerned officers to seemingly ruthless villains was not an easy change to bear.

Furthermore, the shift of decision-making power to a few people at the centre of the stage left many devout officers and councillors feeling alienated and 'out in the cold'. Morale was bound to suffer and it did. The department became a smaller, tougher and more pressurized culture in which to work. There grew a feeling of fighting to survive in a constant state of crisis.

The lowered morale was not restricted to shire hall. It was also apparent in the schools throughout the county. This was discussed at length in Chapter 3 but it is worth recalling here that morale was placed at the top of the list of concerns of heads in nearly all schools which replied to the questionnaire in 1983. With the industrial action extending into 1985 there is little doubt that these concerns will be even more prominent in the future.

In summary, it is possible to take the remarks from the above paragraphs and apply them to Shire as a whole. The crisis culture left no section untouched. The new situation brought about by the continual demand for savings coupled with constant uncertainty produced a profound change in the way (to paraphrase Handy, 1976) work is organized, authority is exercised and people are rewarded and controlled. For most of those involved the change was not for the better. To live by crisis for too long can only produce demoralized services. But is it possible to adapt? Could there evolve a cuts culture in which contraction is anticipated and planned for as a matter of routine? This idea is examined in Part III.

PART III

Towards a Cuts Culture?

An advertisement for *The Times* newspaper shows Julius Caesar gazing contentedly towards the horizon whilst behind him, plotting with heads together, are a group of white-robed assassins. The caption reads: 'Don't you wish you were better informed?'

The Law Society provides a poster for display in solicitors' offices. It reads: 'Making a will won't kill you.'

These two statements embody important values and attitudes directly relevant to the research question which began this study. Can organizations plan and participate in their own decline? The first statement relates to the need for information in order to avert future problems or even disasters. The means to do this, or at least to do it in a more effective way than at present in the crisis culture, already exist.

But doing it and acting upon the information are a very different matter. This relates to the second statement. A cuts culture would have to overcome some of these 'implementation' problems and be able to plan its own contraction when the need arose.

The mixed attitudes associated with making a will are not easily shed as the days of confidently anticipated growth are left behind – perhaps for ever. Such attitudes are embodied in traditional structures of organizations and in the actions and feelings of the individuals who are part of them. A cuts culture is by definition one which plans its own contraction but avoids many of the problems faced by the crisis culture. There are signs of the emergence of such a culture in Shire. It may never go beyond an embryo stage; perhaps it never should. But it is both interesting and informative to examine what seems to be happening and to speculate what might happen if the trend were to be carried to its logical conclusion.

In Chapter 8 the inevitable struggles associated with the emergence of such a culture are explored, and some conclusions are drawn. In Chapter 9 some speculations are made as to possible radical alternatives which could, in theory, occur.

8

An Emerging Cuts Culture?

A cuts culture is not associated with termination (as when a company is officially wound up), nor is it related to major axeing of parts of an organization such as plant closures made by British Steel or pit closures by the Coal Board. Rather, it is a culture which is linked to extended periods of marginal contraction. In some respects it might be likened to a crisis culture except that uncertainty is no longer accompanied by very short decision-time. Crises may still intrude into the cuts culture, yet, overall, there is time for reflection, review, evaluation and negotiation. The future may not look bright, but at least there is the opportunity to prepare for it.

The cuts culture will not, in its emergent stage, be a stable culture. It is likely to contain three competing elements, which are called here defensive, pragmatic and reformist.

The first, defensive, looks to the past, and from this element will come resistance to change and attempts to reinstate cuts made earlier. The second, pragmatic, represents those forces within the organization which, although not unsympathetic towards the defensive element, seek ways to deal with a generally unpleasant but seemingly unavoidable condition. The third, reformist, looks to the future and to the kind of major shifts in aims, attitudes, structures and procedures which seem necessary in order to adapt to major environmental changes – see Figure 8.1.

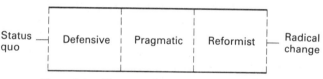

Figure 8.1   *Elements of an emerging cuts culture*

127

An emerging cuts culture will experience all three elements but with the defensive and reformist acting in opposition to each other. This will tend to create a climate of dissent, rancour, conflict, instability and inflexibility.

The effects of having to deal with cuts can also be seen at the individual level where many of those involved will experience, within themselves, defensiveness, pragmatism and the desire for reform. The competing aims, expectations and values associated with this experience will often lead to stress and seemingly uncharacteristic behaviour on the part of those involved.

A more mature cuts culture, however, would have moved some way towards a reformist position. The defenders would, for all practical purposes, have succumbed to the will of the reformers. Similarly, individuals would have adjusted to change and overcome immobilizing, internal defence mechanisms. This is the situation considered in Chapter 9.

The three elements of the 'emergent' cuts culture and their implications for policy-making are now considered.

(1) The Defensive Element

There is a major element of defensiveness in the crisis culture, and in that situation the forces opposed to contraction will play their part in influencing policy decisions. But by its very nature the crisis culture is precipitated towards immediately feasible solutions which will ensure short-term survival. Unless the defensive forces are very powerful they will be overruled by those who are accorded the power to deal with the emergency. In the crisis situation they are less likely to be influential than in the early stages of a cuts culture.

As the cuts become a feature of organizational life, more and more aspects of the valued past will be examined in a relatively unhurried way which will permit the development of pre-planned and, possibly, organized resistance. Both the providers and the receivers of services will be reminded of the importance of various needs that 'have to be' met and of the standards of service 'necessary' to satisfy them adequately.

Defensiveness becomes a particularly important influence when political and professional interests coincide. They stem from different sources but are committed to a similar end – opposition to the cuts.

Political opposition may arise primarily from party ideology. The left and centre are, by and large, committed to growth and improvement in local government services. Resistance to change geared towards contraction is, therefore, predictable. The Labour group in Shire, as in most other authorities, does not disguise its policy of opposition to all cuts in the education service and its demand for immediate reinstatement of past cuts. The rhetoric opposing the cuts tends to grow in volume and sophistication in the early stages of the culture and may be converted into demonstration and action, particularly if various opposing interest groups can be brought together.

The fight to save small schools is a case in point. The higher cost of small schools compared to larger ones is not in dispute; some have a unit cost per pupil of over twice the average. To maintain them is to deprive larger, urban schools of much needed resources. The curriculum is necessarily restricted, and pupils will have contact with a very limited number of staff – possibly only two.

Despite this, there are social reasons for maintaining them. They are an important part of village life. Young children, it can be argued, should grow up close to their own community and not be transported miles away for their education. The emotional security which they derive from being close to home and amongst people they know well outweighs the apparent educational disadvantages of smallness, which are difficult to prove anyway.

But whatever the logical or emotional arguments involved, the defenders must object to the closure: it is a cut and must, therefore, be resisted. One councillor interviewed admitted that, on rational grounds, he could see the reason for closing a school within his area but he had to oppose it. He encouraged people in the locality to fight for their school, to write letters to Shire Hall and to the press, to organize protest meetings and to invite officers to the school to hear the arguments against closure. He lobbied members of education and its subcommittees, especially the added members who held a balance of (voting) influence. He involved the MP for the area and encouraged church dignitaries to write to the Chairman of Education adding their weight to the opposition. He also analysed demographic trends and put forward a case for delay on the grounds of a possible population increase in the near future. The immediate threat was lifted, although perhaps only temporarily.

The political right may also be drawn into opposing major cuts but for different reasons to the left. For the right, particularly a traditionally independent right as in Shire, local autonomy is an important principle. Government guidance is acceptable, but ever increasing government interference in local affairs is not. The cuts may, up to a point, be regarded as desirable, but the restrictions imposed upon the manoeuvrability deemed necessary to deal with such cuts are not. Resistance is geared towards preserving autonomy not to perpetuating growth.

The loss of autonomy is also reflected in the defensiveness of professional officers and the departments to which they belong. Resistance to contraction is many-faceted and complex. On a personal level the growth of a service means more opportunities and, potentially, better career prospects. Contraction means not only less opportunities but also the possibility of actual job loss.

More altruistically, growth is seen to mean the provision of a better service, quantitatively and qualitatively, for the client.

The personal and professional motives may come together in the organizational in-fighting for resources. Here the motive is departmental status, autonomy and size relative to other departments. Why should one department lose out to the benefit of another?

The schools, too, attempt to create their own defences, some of which were described in Chapters 2 and 3. Walsh *et al.* (1983), analysing the effects of falling rolls on schools, suggest that headteachers will aim 'to avoid change rather than to plan for long-term decline which is in any case difficult given uncertainties over future pupil and staff numbers and perhaps the existence of the school itself. Thus planning is frequently negative rather than positive. Heads are forced into solutions that are expedient rather than desirable' (p. 202).

Defensiveness, then, is a powerful, natural and complex force. It combines rational and emotional arguments, and the distinction between selfish and altruistic motives is often lost in the rhetoric. Sacred cows and white elephants are mixed in with essential work-horses. It is the function of the reformist element in the cuts culture to sort out this menagerie. Defensiveness and reform are incompatible elements in the culture, and the opposing pulls which they generate makes the culture a difficult one in which to work. In between, and providing an essential balance, is the pragmatic element discussed next.

(2) The Pragmatist Element

'Somebody has to make the difficult and unpleasant decisions,' remarked one senior officer, and a similar statement was made by a councillor and education committee member. They both felt that they had committed themselves to an unpalatable course of action and both expressed the view that there seemed no other alternative; they were forced to make the best of a bad situation.

This is individual pragmatism, but the exact origins of the decision to which they referred and the process which led to it were not so easily traced. Many individuals, groups, departments and committees were involved. Ultimately the decision might be put down to corporate pragmatism – a form of action much easier for participants to comply with and one which helps them deal with the internal stress caused by the competing pulls of defensiveness and the need for substantial reform.

In the incident referred to, a report had been prepared by a senior officer on a sensitive issue to do with school closures, and this was agreed by the chairman of the main committee concerned. The matter was referred to committee and then to a subcommittee, which set up a working party to investigate the matter further. The working party consulted various local interest groups and reported back to the subcommittee, setting out the difficulties involved in the proposed solution. It was assumed that members would discuss the findings and either ask for more information or make their own decision on the evidence available. The subcommittee, however, simply endorsed the working party's findings and tentative solution, on the assumption that careful groundwork had already been done, and passed the decision to the parent committee. The higher the matter went through the various committees, the more constrained members felt in questioning the decision of the lower committees, where it was felt the detailed work should already have been done. One opposition spokesman who queried the matter in a higher committee was told by the chairman that this committee 'should not have to go through all that again'.

This receding locus of responsibility (see Noble and Pym, 1970) is an important part of the management of decline in a cuts culture. It helps to smooth the path for the decision-makers and enables them to act pragmatically whilst still, explicitly or implicitly, accepting the need for defence and the restoration of cuts. The responsibility for the decision is placed upon a corporate will rather than an individual commitment.

But there may be another reason why people act pragmatically, seemingly against their own values and beliefs. Billings, Milburn and Schaalman (1980) refer to a phenomenon which they call 'emotional inoculation'. It is related to the element of surprise and the time available for reaction. Where there is considerable surprise, the perception of crisis will be high, and this will provoke crisis reactions as described in Chapter 7. However, when the negative event is anticipated in advance, there is time to search for and, sometimes, find reassuring information. By accepting this information, members of the organization, as a group, inoculate themselves against experiencing the negative effects of their decision.

The process may be similar at an organizational level to the personal, psychological defence of 'rationalization' in which an individual's definition and interpretation of an unpleasant event change in order to cope with the situation. The reasoning goes: 'perhaps what is about to happen is necessary anyway, and there are certainly some good features about it'!

This can have a number of effects. For a time, trimming and pruning can provide satisfaction. Officers and members will occasionally compliment themselves or their staff on the 'efficiencies' achieved in areas where previously they had been pledged to resist cuts at all costs. The search for novel solutions can also be generated by the knowledge of impending cuts, and there is an understandable feeling of pleasure and pride when these are found.

Pragmatism in these circumstances is the art of 'the just-about-possible' (and implied in this is the search for a solution which minimizes direct conflict), coupled with the principle of 'least damage', or what a Shire internal report refers to as a 'minimum regret profile, i.e. aiming for a solution that does not antagonise a large section of the community as a greater priority than seeking optimal satisfaction of some minority group'.

The essence of pragmatism in the cuts culture is summed up by Levine (1978) in what he terms retrenchment politics:

> In most cases, however, conflict will not be rancorous, and strategies for dealing with decline will be a mixed bag of tactics intended either to resist or to smooth decline. The logic here is that no organization accedes to cuts with enthusiasm and will try to find a way to resist cuts; but resistance is risky. In addition to the possibility of being charged with non-feasance, no responsible manager wants to be faced with the prospect of being unable to control where the cuts will take place or confront quantum cuts with unpredictable consequences. Instead, managers will choose

a less risky course and attempt to protect organizational
capacity and procedures by smoothing decline and its effects
on the organization.

(p. 320)

The link here between the defensive and the pragmatic is
clear. Underlying the decremental action is a psychological
resistance but it is a resistance which has to be repressed or
'inoculated'. 'What has to be done has to be done' is the
prevailing attitude, but the path must be made as smooth as
possible. This leads to a number of tactics which Levine
(1978) lists. He includes, for instance, the following under
the heading 'Tactics to smooth decline' (p. 321):

Cut low prestige programmes. Cut programmes to politically weak clients. Cut programmes run by weak sub-units.
Shift programmes to another agency. Renegotiate long-term
contracts to regain flexibility. Mortgage the future by deferring maintenance and down-scaling personnel quality. Ask
employees to make voluntary sacrifices like taking early
retirement and deferring rises. Sell surplus property and
lease back when needed.

Many of these tactics have been used in Shire. A number
have been applied, in one way or another, to schools in
general and, for instance, school meals in particular.

The subject of 'managing in hard times' has become a
topical one in local authority journals, and many suggestions
and examples are offered which fall within the ambit of
pragmatism. Kemp (1983), for instance, looks to California
and lists a number of ideas which 'innovative management'
should consider. He preludes his examples with the following statement:

Where to reduce cost? How to increase productivity? What
fees and user charges can be increased? These questions have
forced government officials to look for 'targets of opportunity', scanning the organization to see where opportunities
exist to accomplish the task.

(p. 2)

Some of these 'targets of opportunity' mentioned by Kemp are familiar in Shire, for instance: shared purchasing; reductions in central staff; reduced employee benefits; private use of public facilities; employee suggestion programmes; reduced cleaning services; shared equipment; private sector financial support.

The essence of this form of 'hard times management' is its piecemeal and *ad hoc* nature. It moves from one temporary solution to the next in order to minimize disruption. In so doing, the sense of purpose and mission which provides the underlying rationale for each service is lost, and they become ends in themselves gradually losing their shape and focus. To counteract this the cuts culture seeks a more reformist approach concerned less with smoothing the path than with identifying new directions.

(3)   The Reformist Element

As planned growth is to *laissez-faire* expansion, the reformist element of the cuts culture is to defensiveness and pragmatism. Some of the techniques described in connection with planned growth are potentially usable here but they meet with a very different situation. Planning for contraction involves considerable problems not only in identifying potential areas for contraction but also in implementing policy decisions against the defensiveness which is not normally found in the planned growth culture.

The techniques of analysis likely to be used by the reformist element in the cuts culture depend upon the view taken of the role of local government. It can be argued, following Stewart (1983a), that because an authority is a political entity concerned with the affairs of a specific community it is more than simply a provider of services. It also has, within limits, a considerable say in what those services should be, how and to whom they should be provided and under what conditions. It has the potential to be an active rather than a passive provider and, besides responding to needs, can also identify and promote change, thereby stimulating new needs.

It is also concerned with the future as well as the present and should, therefore, attempt to predict, plan and influence events according to predetermined policies. Analysis may, therefore, take various forms. Four forms are considered here: strategic, functional, issues and performance analysis.

(a) Strategic Analysis

The focus here is outwards towards the community served in an attempt to identify and assess its present and future needs and problems. This is a scanning exercise; a pulling together of the many needs and problems with which the community must grapple now and in the future. It involves thinking about priorities and about change. The task is considerable and in a time of scarce resources it can add a further heavy burden to an already overloaded administration.

Greenwood *et al.* (1976) define 'strategic analysis' as the collection of information and the preparation of data covering the local authority as a whole in order to provide the context within which detailed policy and financial decisions are taken. According to Hinings *et al.* (1980) it may take any of the following forms:

1. preparation of a profile of the social, economic and physical circumstances of the local authority;
2. preparation of a summary statement of the activities of the Council;
3. preparation of new kinds of budgets, including multi-year expenditure projections to show the trend and determinants of Council expenditure; and
4. the arrangement of financial data to facilitate policy planning, rather than for purposes of financial control.

(p. 77)

Such forms of analysis require careful forethought and organization. They break with tradition and override normal departmental boundaries. They require an interdisciplinary approach and a futuristic outlook. Apart from any question as to how, eventually, to use the reports which provide broad and probably unfamiliar scenarios, they are, in themselves, processes which demand imagination and creativity as well as the use of various survey and quantitative techniques.

(b) Functional Analysis

Paralleling strategic analysis, the authority will be concerned to analyse its own functioning. Is it doing what it should be doing? Can it adequately respond to immediate needs and has it the means to predict and cope with future pressures? Are its separate units adequately co-ordinated and geared towards the attainment of corporate goals?

These are difficult questions to answer and still more difficult to do anything about. The answers may well challenge the status quo and provoke strong resistance from vested interests. Tinkering with organizational structures, setting up new committees or cross-departmental working parties, opening up new information channels, or providing alternative budgetary procedures may all help in a small way but they are closer to the pragmatic solutions referred to earlier. What the reformist element in the cuts culture is concerned with are more radical changes possibly involving major restructuring of services and the means whereby they are administered and controlled.

Spencer (1984), considering alternative forms of service provision by local authorities, raises some important distinctions. Traditionally councils have accepted a triple role in providing a service. They have planned it, financed it and produced and distributed it. The only alternative normally put forward, and one which has considerable political overtones, is 'privatization' in which the service, or part of it, is taken over by a separate profit-making organization. Spencer argues that this need not be the case. An authority might decide to perform any or all of the three functions – planning, financing and producing/distributing – in connection with any service falling within its ambit. Similarly it may have the option of 'contracting out' of any or all of these. He continues:

Where the local authority chooses not to undertake all three
of these activities in relation to a service, or part of it, it may
use a range of other agencies to undertake that aspect of the
service which it does not undertake itself. These other
agencies would include:

1. Other public bodies.
2. Private firms.
3. Voluntary bodies.
4. Co-operatives.

(p. 15)

An analysis of these possibilities is bound to raise problems. It will be necessary to consider statutory obligations
and responsibilities, political and ideological objections, and
departmental and professional interests. Underlying many
of these is the question of control. Traditionally the authority has controlled all aspects of the service but, as Spencer
(1984) points out, full control is expensive and often bears a
heavy opportunity cost. Other productive aspects of a
service may have to be reduced as control is increased. Also,
a contract need not mean completely contracting out; it can
involve a range of co-operative ventures in which control is
shared, and the authority maintains a monitoring or super-
visory role.

It is clear that such ideas carry with them the seeds of
radical change. The shape of local government organizations
could be very different. Their structures, modes of operating
and financing would be unlike anything previously experienced. But in the reformist element of the cuts culture such
thinking is expected. In Shire, for instance, an internal
discussion paper put forward the idea that instead of regarding county council departments as a corporate entity they
should be looked at as a set of companies:

Each would have its own Board of Directors but there would
be one controlling company whose Board was made up of
Managing and some other Directors from the other Boards.
Each 'company' would not necessarily be one Department
but a cluster of Departments with a high level of mutual

communication. The major parts of Education, Libraries and parts of Social Services would be one obvious grouping.

This illustration may seem far removed from existing reality and from the possibility of implementation, but it does represent the kind of thinking which challenges the defensive and pragmatic elements of the culture.

(c) Issues Analysis

At a more specific level the authority will seek to analyse particular problems (as distinct from the broader issues discussed above) occurring, or likely to occur, in its environment. Hinings *et al.* (1980) call this 'issues analysis'. It is more restricted in both scale and scope than 'strategic analysis' but it also has as its underlying concern the collection and presentation of information that will 'facilitate the making of informed and responsible choices between alternative claims upon resources'.

As an example the authors take 'care of the elderly' as an issue which one local authority analysed in this way. The issue was divided into six key topic areas: client group statistics; housing and accommodation; domestic services; social contact and leisure activity; health; and poverty.

One of the key tasks of the analysis was to uncover a 'needs-provision gap' in any of the areas. Needs were to be derived from an assessment of 'standard needs' based upon approved national and/or professional standards, or 'local needs' which reflected the circumstances of the community served. Identification of a 'gap' would normally be followed by a consideration of alternative courses of action, perhaps accompanied by some form of cost-benefit analysis, or in-depth studies of matters of particular concern.

An important point about issues analysis is that it normally crosses departmental boundaries and is related to several services, some of which may fall outside of the domain of the county council. In the above example, social services, housing, leisure, health and social security, plus possibly education and libraries, could all be involved.

The problem of needs and standards is also raised in this form of analysis, and this is particularly important in the fourth category of analysis which concerns itself with the performance of individual services.

(d) Performance Analysis

Using performance analysis the authority examines its current service provision. Is it of the right kind? Are the standards appropriate? Is each service effective and efficient? Is the service available to those who need it at a price they can afford? Is it responsive to changing needs and demands? These are some of the questions that an analysis of this kind will seek to answer. The approaches used fall under the general heading of what Cronbach *et al.* (1980) call 'programme evaluation'.

Programme analysis and review, value for money, performance review and cost-effectiveness analysis are some of the approaches used by a number of authorities, including Shire.

Cheshire County Council was one of the first to use external management consultants to carry out a major value-for-money study which included a detailed examination of the education service (CBI, 1979). Shire has preferred to carry out such studies internally, but it is clear from two reports (*Resource Plan 1985/86* and *The Next Five Years 1984–1989*) that the process is regarded as an important and continuing one which in future will be co-ordinated by the County Secretary:

> The significant work at present being done to ensure value for money will continue by means of both formal performance review and less formal departmental exercises.
>
> (*Resource Plan*, p. 7)

> The likelihood is that the use of 'in-house' resources would achieve much the same results as external consultants, provided those involved had a clear brief and management support for their activities. Indeed there is a considerable case for setting up such studies as a pre-emptive, positive move to examine potential savings.
>
> (*The Next Five Years*, p. 12)

Local authorities also face a new form of scrutiny based upon comparative statistical analysis which stems from central government's requirement that detailed statistics for all services be published annually. This is backed up by the establishment of the Audit Commission for Local Authorities, concerned with the efficient use of resources in local government.

The Chartered Institute of Public Finance and Accountancy in 1984 issued guidelines to authorities on value-for-money studies and the kinds of indicators of performance which might be used in various services including education.

As a result of these activities there has been a considerable increase in the amount of information available to the public through annual reports and budgets. The Shire budget book for 1984/5, for instance, contains 145 pages of which 35 are devoted entirely to education in the county.

The special adviser to the Chief Secretary to the Treasury published a report (Lord, 1983) relating to educational expenditure and focussed on the question, 'which local authorities appear to be more efficient at turning money into resources, and which are more inefficient?' The results of the analysis show amongst other things that teacher costs per school vary between £8,000 and £11,000 in primary schools in different authorities and £8,800 and £11,200 in secondary schools. The author suggests that:

> Too often more money is naively equated with more 'education'. Although it is more difficult to measure the outputs of education than its inputs, education committees and their officers would do better to spend more time thinking about the quality of the product, even if they found consensus more difficult, than simply about cash flow.
>
> (p. 22)

Many authorities are now engaged in a process of self-analysis on a scale not previously envisaged and involving 'reformers' both inside and outside of local government. But they face a major problem. Feeding the results back into the system and bringing about change are difficult, and the problem is compounded when the evaluation is motivated by a desire to make savings.

There is another problem connected with the evaluation of programmes undertaken by service departments. Most are, to a large extent, based upon professional standards – sometimes laid down explicitly by legislation and sometimes recommended through professional codes of practice. Over time their acceptance gives to them a mantle of immutability. To question them, particularly from the outside, is for most professionals a challenge to professional competence and invokes strong resistance.

But it is these standards which determine the cost base for most services, and without the possibility of questioning their appropriateness the reformist element of the cuts culture is thwarted. It is over the question of standards, as well as goals, priorities and organizational structures, that the internal conflicts in the cuts culture arise.

What is now emerging for most authorities as resources become scarcer is the problem of rationing. This is indicated by the concluding statement in the Shire *Resource Plan 1985/86*:

> To attempt to maintain services at the same level and to provide them in the same way will inevitably result in unplanned reductions in standards, increased justifiable complaints and it will mean that staff will be placed under excessive pressures. Public confidence in the County Council will be eroded.
>
> It is clearly necessary for there to be a planned approach to contain services within the County's available resources.
>
> (p. 8)

This is a clear statement from the reformist element of the cuts culture but it leaves open the key questions, How should the planned approach be achieved, who should control the process and what are the implications for the future, especially for education? Alternative answers to these questions are considered in the final chapter.

To summarize the main points relating to the emerging cuts culture, it seems that, with a growing certainty of uncertainty, authorities have the opportunity to plan for their contraction in a much more positive way than in the crisis culture. Their task, however, is a difficult one, and the culture faces conflict brought about by the opposing pulls of those seeking to defend the status quo and those seeking more radical reforms. In between, trying to smooth the path towards decline, are the pragmatists who themselves are torn between preserving and changing – 'but somebody has to do the job'. In one sense the cuts culture might seem to function more 'effectively' if the reformers were to gain greater power than the defenders. If this happens various tools of analysis will be used to re-define goals and procedures and to question long-established professional norms and standards. But where would these lead? Some speculations are made in Chapter 9.

9

Towards a Mature Cuts Culture?

The mature cuts culture probably does not exist but it can be imagined. In its extreme form, and dominated by the reformist element, it would be a well-planned, highly ordered culture; comprehensive in its assessment of needs and diligent in its ordering of priorities. It would be efficient in its use of resources and meticulous in its evaluation of results. For some it would offer the best solution for coping with decline, whilst others might see shades of Orwell or Skinner.

In this chapter it is proposed to explore some real situations and some hypothetical ones in order to create the feeling of what a mature cuts culture might be like and the way in which individual services might be affected. As a lead into this it will be useful to consider what is involved in bringing about radical change in long-established professional services. An analogy with an iceberg is suggested.

The Professional Iceberg

There are two reasons for choosing an iceberg as an analogy for the closely integrated sets of norms, values and methods which go to make up professional (best) practice. An iceberg is densely packed, largely impenetrable and free-floating, and the larger it gets the more difficult it is to change its course. It can be destroyed using considerable force, but minor assaults will leave it virtually unchanged in form.

The second connection is largely theoretical and relates to the work on social change pioneered by Kurt Lewin in the 1950s but developed more recently in relation to educational change by Berg and Östergren (1977). In this approach the

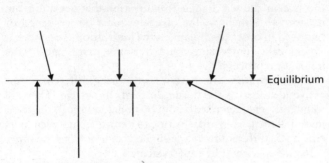

Figure 9.1 *The social force field*

change situation is regarded as a 'social force field' made up
of a number of interacting vectors, which, having different
strengths and directions, eventually provide a relative stability or equilibrium for the system. The idea is generally
accepted as an important part of systems theory. It can be
illustrated simply – see Figure 9.1.

The arrows in the figure illustrate vectors which have both
force and direction. They are, in effect, forces for or against
a particular change, and together they maintain the status
quo, represented by the central line. An analysis using this
concept can be made of any organizational situation which
is faced with the possibility of change. A change of equilibrium in the field requires an increase in the strength of the
vectors on one side or a decrease on the other. Thus, for
instance, in the analysis of a force field, a decrease in money
available to support the status quo, or an increase in parental
pressure to keep open a school threatened with closure,
could mark a change in the vectors impinging on the field.

Berg and Östergren (1977) make the following comments
with regard to innovations introduced into the field:

The innovation may be introduced from the environment,
complete or almost complete. In other cases, ideas or trends
may enter the system from the environment and stimulate
the creation of innovation within the system. But how can

the system allow a change or innovation that deviates from its norms? Somehow, the obstacles must be weakened or removed in order to implement the innovation. This is what Lewin calls 'unfreezing', and it is the first stage of the innovation process.

The innovators are the ones who bring different, innovative ideas across the border lines of the system. They are frequently characterised as oppositional, atypical, different marginal men. They may belong to a subsystem which in its entirety is different from the supersystem or from the other subsystems within the supersystem.

(p. 105)

The first point of interest is the idea of unfreezing and hence the analogy with an iceberg. To bring about change in any substantial form the iceberg must be unfrozen and then, to continue with Lewin's theory, must be refrozen in its new form. The second point is that the unfreezing process is often brought about by people who are not part of the system to which the change is introduced.

These two points, together, raise important questions relating to the large-scale reforms which would be necessary to 'unfreeze' education, change it and then institutionalize the change through 'refreezing'. Who would introduce the reforms? What form would they take, and who would control the process? These questions will be considered shortly, but first it will be useful to consider the case of social services, a system which is in the process of reform. There are some issues here for those involved with education to ponder.

Unfreezing Social Services

In Shire, the social services department has gained something of a reputation as a helpful collaborator in terms of reducing expenditure. It seems, to those interviewed, that the department has, when requested, always managed to find substantial savings despite increasing case-loads. Why should this be?

A senior officer in social services indicated a possible reason, and it is one that clearly illustrates the unfreezing process. It relates to a changing philosophy leading to a shift from a belief in institutional care to a greater acceptance of community care. In practice, many homes and other welfare units providing long-term care have been closed down. Since 1977 there has been a steady stream of closures; in some years amounting to fifteen or more. The buildings are sold or used for other purposes, staff are redeployed or retired early, and net savings of up to £50,000 are possible from each closure.

What exactly is this new philosophy, and what has brought it about? Jones, Brown and Bradshaw (1983) provide a useful potted history of the development of community care in the United Kingdom, the main points of which are as follows.

The Royal Commission on Mental Health and Mental Deficiency reported in 1957 on the problem of outdated mental hospitals. The term 'community care' was first officially used in this report, and the rights and obligations of local authorities to provide pre-care and after-care were spelled out. Some impetus to the movement was given by Enoch Powell's speech in 1961 in which he announced a major run-down of mental hospital provision.

In 1962 the Ministry of Health produced a booklet, *Health and Welfare: The Development of Community Care*. This suggested that the emphasis in hospitals should be on acute care; non-acute problems would be dealt with in the community. Those mainly affected would be the physically and mentally handicapped, the mentally ill, geriatric patients and women in childbirth. The idea of community care had thus been extended to include several categories of those needing care.

From another and totally non-economic perspective, there was a growing attack by a number of sociologists on the debilitating effects on patients of 'institutionalization'. Irving Goffman (1961) led the way with *Asylums*, following which there were several critical books including Townsend's *The Last Refuge* (1962), Morris's *Put Away* (1969),

Miller and Gwynne's *A Life Apart* (1972), and King *et al.*, *Patterns of Residential Care* (1972).

At about the same time there were several public inquiries into conditions in various mental hospitals and old people's homes, some of which, e.g. Ely, Farleigh and Whittingham, became widely known through newspaper publicity. Cruelty, ill treatment, poor living conditions and low staff morale were all alleged and investigated.

This publicity, combined with the more analytic and theoretical approach of the sociologists, brought about a shift in both public and professional opinion as to how people should be cared for. During the early 1970s, when there was still the possibility of growth, some changes, mainly the construction of day centres, were implemented; but the motives which lay behind them were mixed. The position is summed up by Jones, Brown and Bradshaw (1983) as follows:

> To the politician, 'community care' is a useful piece of rhetoric; to the sociologist it is a stick to beat institutional care with; to the civil servant, it is a cheap alternative to institutional care which can be passed to the local authorities for action – inaction; to the visionary, it is a dream of the new society in which people really do care; to social service departments, it is a nightmare of heightened public expectations and inadequate resources to meet them. We are only just beginning to find out what it means to the old, the chronic sick and the handicapped.
>
> (p. 102)

Despite these mixed motives many professionals in the social services were convinced by the strength of the case for community care. There have, since the mid-1970s, been numerous developments, including day services for the elderly, mentally handicapped, physically handicapped, mentally ill, elderly confused, family, and offenders. According to Carter (1981) these are mainly provided by social service departments (47 per cent), area health authorities (26 per cent), voluntary organizations (23 per cent) and other statutory providers including education departments (4 per cent). There are also a number of developments involving collaboration between two or more of these providers.

Jones, Brown and Bradshaw (1983), whilst not uncritical of the dangers involved, end on an optimistic note:

> The client keeps his independence and self-respect; the social services are in touch with him and can provide for his needs; and the cost to the statutory services is considerably lower than that of the most minimal kind of institutional care.
>
> Such developments reflect the growing tendency to move on from the polarised, and limited, debate of institutional care versus community care. The emphasis is much more on seeing what kind of care for what kind of patient/resident client in what kind of circumstances is most appropriate. There has developed a sensitive appreciation of the relationship between types of structures and caring skills, and a growing awareness of the political implications of the administrative setting in which such facilities are provided.
>
> (p. 113)

The unfreezing process in the social services was a profound one affecting the very essence of care for those in need. It involved a shift away from the idea that those who proved to be 'special cases', for one reason or another, not conforming to community norms, should be removed from that community until 'restored to normality'. The reformist ideal was based upon the notion that they should be cared for within the community and with the help of that community. As a result the entire concept of care opened up and became fluid.

Costs were no longer solely calculated on unit cost per bed or per place. There was room for radical innovation involving new kinds of purpose-built (hopefully) more efficient small centres, co-operation with other bodies within and outside of the local authority ambit and encouragement for the growth of support networks of various kinds within the community. Total costs may not fall by a large percentage, but the range and flexibility of services can be increased and substantially modified to meet changing needs.

This more optimistic picture need not obscure the possibility of an excessively cost-conscious authority using the unfreezing process to 'dump' those in need 'from the home into the bus shelter', as some critics suggest. Indeed this problem is recognized by those providing the services, and there is some concern as to how easily this could happen – even if, until the present at least, it may not have happened in Shire.

The Education Iceberg

Education may have experienced a short thaw in the 1960s, but the unfreezing process did not reach the centre of the iceberg, which remained solid and unmoved despite some local variations in climate associated with the anti-school and free school movement.

The centre of the iceberg is compacted by a set of traditional norms which imply that education between 5 and 16 years of age mainly takes place in schools, in classrooms, in groups of around thirty, for periods of about forty minutes, for five days a week, for forty weeks a year, studying about six to eight core subjects and some additional options, all of which generally lead to set examinations and certification at the end of the schooling period. The process is largely controlled by a group of professionally trained graduates all paid according to a nationally agreed scale and all spending approximately 80 per cent of their time at the school in the classroom. Each school operates within strict financial regulations laid down by the local authority and is inspected from time to time by officials from central and local government to ensure, amongst other things, that there is no major deviance from the norms. All children must attend school unless a special case can be made for providing alternative education.

Although local authorities and schools pride themselves on their autonomy and freedom from external interference, there is an extraordinary adherence to the norm. Most schools are entirely predictable in terms of the above stereotype. Since the mid-1970s the same could not be said of social services provision.

The majority of schools differ from each other only in terms of minor variations in curriculum, support services and extra-curricular activities, and it is these differences which are disappearing with the cuts.

The two key elements involved in maintaining the stereotype are: best professional standards; and uniformity. These come in for some searching scrutiny by Stewart (1977), writing about local government management in an era of restraint. In connection with standards he writes:

> To challenge the relevance of the national standard is to challenge the relevance of professional best practice. But in an era of economic restraint local authorities have to face the fact that maybe they can no longer afford best professional practice, because best professional practice itself reflects the aspirations of a world of growth. Best professional practice may mean waste, if it does not reflect the authority's priority need.
>
> (p. 12)

Turning to education, he continues:

> The increase in teachers to reduce pupil–teacher ratio reflects understandable ideals. It reflects the desire for ever higher standards of education. It reflects best professional practice . . . But best professional practice can be a bad guide to priorities in a period of restraint.
>
> (p. 12)

> The meaning and significance of standards must be probed and probed deeply. The standard does not justify itself.
>
> (p. 13)

The second issue is that of uniformity; that is, the desire to provide an equivalence of service throughout the area. This also can be wasteful if it is not related to need:

A local authority aims to achieve a uniform standard of service; national and professional standards drive it to that end; and local aspirations support that drive. There is waste, however, in uniformity of service, if need is not uniform within the area served. There is a waste in over-provision, as there is hardship in under-provision. Uniformity of service is an easy target, for it avoids the hard work of analysing how need clusters and varies.

To challenge the assumptions of national standards, of best professional practice or of uniformity of service is necessary if the wider scanning of local authority activities is to open up policy space. The judgements made will be political judgements, and this is how it should be.

. . . The challenge is made not to achieve a cut-back in service, but to provide the opportunity for growth in achievement. The hard test is to compare existing services with what might be; the hard test is to compare the problems being met with the problems not being met.

(p. 14)

This represents a typical reformist statement and, as with so many of the statements of this kind, they are made by the outsider, the 'oppositional, atypical, different, marginal man'. In the mature cuts culture they may be heard and acted upon, but what in such a culture would it mean to 'open up policy space', especially with regard to education?

Unfreezing Education

Stewart (1977) suggests some questions which might be asked in connection with the opening up of policy space, and these are relevant to education within a mature cuts culture:

Who benefits from the service? Who uses it? How widely is it used? Does its usage vary from area to area? Why do these variations occur? Should the service be based on uniformity?

On what are existing levels of activity based? If it is a national standard or a professional standard, on what is it based? How relevant is that standard given local circumstances and present resources?

What damage would be caused if the service were cut? How does the damage occur over time? Is the damage critical? Is it temporary or does it harm life chances?

(p. 14)

It is possible to construct a more specific set of questions which might be directed towards education, for instance:

Does so much education need to take place in school? Could more use be made of the community in which the school is based? Could the school provide more for the community and the community more for the school? Do all communities require the same inputs? Are there cases for special priority?

Does so much teaching need to take place in classrooms and in groups of a standard size? Are alternative teaching methods possible, and might pupils be given more responsibility for their own learning or for helping each other?

Need so many subjects be taught and/or need they be taught for so many periods, for so many years? Need they all be examined?

Why should all teaching be done by trained graduates? Is there room for less-qualified assistant teachers? Should there be more flexibility in the appointment and deployment of the teaching force?

Might not schools be given more responsibility for organizing their own affairs in terms of managing their own finance, their own evaluation and appraisal and their own staff development?

Questions of this kind are not new; they have arisen at different times, for different reasons. Illich (1971) and Goodman (1971), for instance, have raised many of them in their attacks on conventional schooling.

In a very different situation, at a very different time, *The Report on the Curriculum and Organisation of Secondary Schools* (ILEA, 1984) also asks searching questions which challenge existing educational practices and boundaries, for instance:

- What do people expect of the school? What kind of access do they want to it?

- Are there individuals or groups in the community who have a special contribution to make to school life?
- Has the school a special contribution to make to community life?
- How can schools, the youth service and the adult education institutes work more closely together so that young people are involved in all three before the age of 16?
- Might a pupil enrol on an adult education course, either as a substitute for or in addition to a course of study provided by the school?
- Might some adult students enrol in school classes for public examinations? Would not the presence of adults in school classes have beneficial effects on the behaviour and motivation of some pupils? Would this not lead to the more efficient use of resources?
- Might it not be advantageous for teachers to be involved in teaching both school pupils and adults? Have not schools much to learn from the traditions and methods of adult education? Are the problems which inhibit such overlap and cross-fertilization really insuperable?

The action which will stem from this report and these searching questions still remains to be seen.

In another context a report by Walsh *et al.* (1984), presenting the findings of a nationwide study of falling rolls and the management of the teaching profession, also raises many questions concerning the inflexibility created by attitudes and practices formed during periods of growth.

They conclude that short-term solutions, many of which tend to protect the status quo, are likely to build up even greater problems in the future. The flexibility needed to manage a contracting situation is inhibited by, amongst other things, attempts to cushion schools and preserve pupil–teacher ratios; by contracts which appoint teachers to schools and not to authorities; by the Burnham points system which is appropriate to a period of growth and not to one of contraction; by a budgetary and financing system which is cumbersome and restricts possible cost-saving initiatives by the schools themselves; and by a rigid defence of a traditional curriculum.

To pose the questions above is enough to raise the water temperature around the iceberg, but this falls far short of the action needed for unfreezing. The questions would have to be answered with radical new solutions and action taken to bring about major changes. For instance, if questions are asked about how schools are financed, and the present methods are found to be cumbersome and inhibiting, one solution might be to give each school considerably more autonomy over its own affairs. Such schemes are already in operation in several authorities, and an advanced form of devolution is being tried in a number of schools in Cambridgeshire and Solihull (Burgess, 1983; Humphrey and Thomas, 1983). They represent a major shift in attitudes towards educational management.

Perhaps the most radical of all the possibilities which might emerge if open policy space were to be used to its fullest extent would be a breaking down of the barriers between education and the community – including other services provided to the community. This possibility is inherent in much of the questioning set out above. It is only when the boundaries are made more permeable that radical change can take place. Here there might be some comparison with the changes taking place in the social services, in so far as it would not simply be a reduction in resources which stimulates the change but a change in professional ideas and values also.

What follows is not a case for community education but a speculation as to the radical changes which might take place in an 'unfreezing' or 'open policy space' situation.

Education and the Community

The argument for community education in a time of contraction might be made along the following lines. Even during periods of sustained growth, education did not entirely match the aspirations and expectations of its clients – pupils, parents, employers and the community. Even more, during a period of financial restraint, the needs of education as a service cannot be considered separately from the needs of the community which it serves. The community should have a say in what is to be cut if cuts have to be made; and consideration should be given to whether, rather than a cut, those affected may not wish to find an alternative – community-supported – means of providing part of the service.

Consideration of the possibility of lessening the barriers between service provision and the community is to be found in authorities politically as far apart as the ILEA (see the questions above) and Shire – although some might allege that their motives were different. In Shire the *Resource Plan 1985/86* devotes almost half of its length to community involvement. It pledges: 'To continue and develop arrangements to encourage and support communities and individuals to take responsibility for themselves and to encourage participation with the County Council in the provision of services' (p. 3).

Community education is far from new. Henry Morris, writing in *New Ideals Quarterly* in 1926, summed up the philosophy: 'We should abolish the barriers which separate education from all those activities which make up adult living.' Fletcher (1980), tracing the development of the movement, summarizes the three guiding principles of community colleges: 'First let all the villagers come to their place; bring them in. Second let education be informed by where it is found; be relevant. Third let facilities be shared; save money' (p. 6).

The final point will not escape the notice of the cost-conscious reformers of today. In more recent times there have been numerous experiments in lessening the barriers between school and community. Several of those that have achieved notoriety have been well documented, e.g. Groby Community College in Poster (1982), Countesthorpe, Codsall, Abraham Moss and Sidney Stringer, amongst others, in Fletcher and Thompson (1980), Countesthorpe and the Sutton Centre in Fletcher, Carron and Williams (1985). The Sutton Centre in the north-east of England, described by Wilson (1980), is almost the antithesis of the stereotype of traditional education set out earlier in this chapter.

The Sutton experience suggests that the school should seek to break down six barriers: those around the educational buildings, the school itself; those put up to other sections of the community; those erected by teachers around themselves as teachers with regard to their teaching role; those around the curriculum; those around the young people, making them different once they step inside; those that exist between head and staff and between departments.

The Sutton Centre school was a controversial one which demanded flexible hours from teachers and encouraged members of the public to attend and to give lessons. There were problems with these ideals, as Wilson himself points out, just as there were problems with Countesthorpe and other radical new ventures. Perhaps too many barriers were taken down too soon?

But then, in the mature cuts culture, other barriers, besides those between schools and the community, would have to be removed. In particular, the barriers between education and the other services provided by the local authority would have to be lowered. The goal of the authority would, in the mature culture, be to identify and satisfy the needs of the community and not simply to provide certain predetermined services. These needs would almost certainly span the various services and demand their co-operation. Policy space would have to be created across, as well as within, departments. Services would lose much of their autonomy.

The 'ideal' mature cuts culture, then, would be community oriented and concerned to take a comprehensive view in the assessment of needs and the ordering of priorities. Education would form but a single, albeit important, strand in the community network.

It must not be forgotten that the culture is built upon the premise of continuing contraction, and despite the good intentions of the reformers there are considerable dangers inherent in the process. These dangers are considered in Chapter 10, and a case is made for matching powerful reforming zeal against carefully managed professional defensiveness.

10

Conclusion: Countervailing Powers

The cuts culture is founded on the premise of contraction. It normally results in a gradual decline in the services available to the community which the local authority serves. In Chapter 9 ways of managing this decline were considered and the possibility of a reformist-dominated culture which might bring about a constructive re-allocation of resources and services was discussed.

In its extreme form a reformist-dominated culture would probably mean some radical changes within the organization. Departmental and professional boundaries would be lowered, and policy-making would become more centralized. Corporate plans would be formulated spanning all services. They would be implemented through a hierarchy based upon a greatly strengthened, if not entirely new, corporate team. The budgetary system would be changed, and again control would shift to the centre – to the administrators away from the professional departments. Historical budgeting would be replaced with zero-based budgeting in which each aspect of expenditure would have to be justified each year.

Overall the structure of a reformist-dominated culture would be very different from the traditional authority. The role of members would become more uncertain, and, as with the officers, power would shift to a few centrally placed people, leaving the rank and file to play their part at the periphery.

The idea of a far-seeing, corporate body facilitating and supporting the community in its efforts to forge a new and comprehensive range of services, despite ever-decreasing central funds, has its attractions, but to the cynic it is pure fantasy. To the shrewd organizational observer it is unworkable, and to the professional, immersed in a local government service, it is anathema.

To the politician, however, intent upon reductions in public expenditure, it is a golden opportunity to bring about ideological change whilst the defenders are uncertain and demoralized. Herein lies the problem of a reformist-dominated cuts culture: it is possible for the reformers to ride roughshod over the defenders. What emerges may indeed be change, even necessary change, but it will usually ignore the benefits and wisdom of traditional practices created through the experience of the professional services.

Klein (1973), discussing resistance to change, argues the importance of the 'defender role' and suggests that:

> a necessary prerequisite of successful change involves the mobilization of forces against it. It [the major thesis of his paper] has suggested that just as individuals have their defenses to ward off threat, maintain integrity, and protect themselves against the unwarranted intrusions of others' demands, so do social systems seek ways in which to defend themselves against ill-considered and overly precipitous innovations.
>
> (p. 120)

He continues by explaining why the defender role is so important to the system faced with major changes:

> Thus an important implication for the change agent is that the defender, whoever he may be and however unscrupulously or irrationally he may appear to present himself and his concerns, usually has something of great value to communicate about the nature of the system which the change agent is seeking to influence.
>
> (p. 122)

In education there are now many examples of changes pushed through without consultation and with little or no regard for the legitimate views of those affected. When the reformers also hold the purse-strings, their power, and therefore their ability to impose change, is greatly increased. This is particularly apparent in education at the present time.

The government's reformist posture has shaken the confidence of many in the education profession. Reform has not been, and is not being, sensitively handled, and all indications point to an attempt to gain much greater central control of the service.

Examples in 1985 of centrally inspired initiatives include, for instance: the annual pay negotiations involving conditions of service and teacher appraisal; the Technical and Vocational Education Initiative; the certificate of prevocational education; the Secretary of State's proposals on the 5-to-16 curriculum and new forms of examination; new approaches to mathematics teaching; the abolition of the Schools Council; the publication of HMI reports; HMI inspection of local authorities; increased expectations of performance; and the establishment of the Audit Commission.

Most worrying of all to those in education is the centrally administered decline, or in some cases re-direction, of resources accompanying these changes.

A specific example of the power of the central reformers is provided by a change in the origin and control of resources and new curriculum developments accompanying vocationally oriented education. In this change, mainly affecting secondary and further education, employers are regarded as the main consumers of educational output. The arguments for this change can be made convincingly, as the following statement by Lord Young (1984), former Chairman of the Manpower Services Commission, indicates:

> Major changes in the structure of industry include the decline of heavy manufacturing; the growth of the service sector; the larger proportion of service-type jobs within the manufacturing sector; and the gradual and continuing reduction in the number of unskilled jobs. Perhaps even more important is the need for higher levels of skill and a broader range of skills to cope with more complex problems arising in the work place.

Within education, the need to respond to changes in society and the labour market has been acknowledged by schools which are seeking to develop and enrich the curriculum in appropriate ways. There has been a growing recognition that young people need to be better able to apply what they have learned in practical situations; to use initiative and co-operate effectively with others in solving problems; to acquire the higher skills required by sophisticated technology; and in particular to know how to learn, since rapid change will require people to acquire new and updated skills more easily.

(p. 8)

This statement is taken from an explanation, in the *Head Teacher's Review*, of the Technical and Vocational Education Initiative (TVEI) for which, in 1984, the Manpower Services Commission made £150 million available. About 100 LEAs, 350 schools and 100 colleges are co-operating in the scheme, which will mean that selected pupils and students will take a more vocationally oriented curriculum than their peers.

The Royal Society of Arts has linked the concept of 'education for capability' with the TVEI scheme and has launched a campaign to encourage interest in vocational capability. The autumn 1984 *Newsletter* (RSA, 1984) sponsored by IBM (United Kingdom) Ltd is devoted to explaining and furthering vocational education.

The recently introduced idea of a certificate of prevocational education for secondary schools, the growing influence of the Business and Technical Education Council's schemes, plus the massive input of skills, resources and innovative ideas into the Youth Training Scheme indicate that 'policy space' can be created for education generally, and that the implications could be far reaching.

In this instance the reformers are mainly outside of the local education authorities, but their influence and resources, exerted through the Manpower Services Commission, are considerable. Where are the defenders, and who will listen to them even if they make a case for caution and put forward arguments which run counter to those of the reformers?

Meanwhile, back in Shire, different, but now familiar, problems are being tackled. Whilst the Manpower Services Commission is wielding its extensive financial power, the situation at the end of 1984, for the primary and secondary sectors after a decade of contraction, was still gloomy. An ominous paper was produced by the Chief Executive in mid-year. It read:

Large scale reductions in expenditure 1985–1988. A Note by the Chief Executive.

1. The reductions in expenditure which may well be needed during this period seem to be very much more than can be achieved by the methods used to date. The savings achieved in recent years have been obtained in part by stopping certain activities but, for the most part, they have been obtained by reducing the scale and standards of activities, improving efficiency and reducing staff numbers through mutually agreed redundancies.

2. It is my view that, whilst these processes will continue to show savings, they will not be able to provide reductions of expenditure of the size which may be necessary. I have, therefore, for the information of the Chairmen, listed a variety of activities across the board which could be stopped or severely reduced in scale. This is not a corporate offering and my colleague chief officers will have views on whether these activities are suitable for savings and over what period . . .

3. I feel it an obligation, however, to make sure that Chairmen are fully aware of the sort of savings which might have to come about if our view of the implications of government policy is correct.

A similar view was put forward by the County Treasurer during an interview in June 1984.

These are not crisis culture views. They are views looking forward and warning of the need for radical change. They are from the reformists within the authority and they alert the service departments to things to come. Implied in their statements is the warning, Unless you can find major savings in ways acceptable to you, then some services will have to be stopped. This is not an empty threat. Unless there is a failure of the corporate, political machinery, then funding for certain programmes can and will be stopped by decision of the council.

The kind of response to this threat indicates the prevailing culture. The Chief Education Officer, in a memorandum to the Chairman of Education, states:

> You will recall that the Chairman of County Council has called a further meeting of Committee Chairmen and Chief Officers . . . at which he wishes to consider 'clear options for substantial savings for 1985/86 onwards together with a report on the implications of such savings . . .'.
>
> Bearing in mind that virtually every reduction in Education expenditure I can suggest to you now must mean a cut in the quality of the service we provide, I feel very diffident about putting up 'clear options' without some indication from the committee of where they would wish these cuts to fall.

The report then lists various areas including school meals, building maintenance, school closures, midday supervision, non-teaching staff, teaching staff, transport and other items which might be cut; potential savings which might be made and the likely effects of such cuts. Three main options are offered: a 1.5 per cent reduction on base budget saving about £2 million; a 2.3 per cent reduction saving nearly £3 million; and a 3.3 per cent cut, saving approximately £4 million.

A further note continues:

> I recognise that education must meet its share of any further savings and that at this stage I see these savings have to be made in three main ways.
>
> (a)   By saving consequent upon falling rolls – what a pity we cannot re-apply some of these savings to improve facilities elsewhere.
>
> (b)   By taking more surplus places out of use and this means closing secondary schools. However, the dilemma here is that we need the Secretary of State's approval to closures.

(c)   I see no alternative for major savings but to look to the School Meals Service . . .

Finally, I see that in the papers for the Chairman and Chief Officers' meeting . . . the Chief Executive has sketched some personal thoughts for areas of provision which are non-statutory and, therefore, could theoretically be reduced or eliminated. He makes it clear these are his personal views and have not been discussed with other Chief Officers. I would take issue with him over the ability of the County Council to make significant reductions in some of the areas listed for Education without infringing our legal obligations.

Within the CEO's response a mixture of pragmatist and defender roles is apparent. The defender points to unavoidable cuts in quality, reiterates that savings from falling rolls should be used to improve facilities, throws back the decision as to where to make cuts to the members and takes issue with the Chief Executive on the question of statutory provision. The pragmatist recognizes that the education service must meet its share of further reductions, suggests a number of options and offers advice as to where further cuts might cause least harm.

Short of outright defiance, what more could he do in these circumstances? The pragmatist realizes that defiance would merely delay matters, and in the long run a decision would be made by outsiders probably resulting in a far less satisfactory solution as far as education was concerned.

The solution may well lie in the acceptance of the importance of defensiveness in the culture as a bulwark against unbridled reformism.

Stewart (1977), after his challenge to professional norms and standards, considers the role of corporate planning as one of the tools of the reformers. He is circumspect in advocating its use. It has a role, he argues, but one very different to that appropriate in a time of growth. New methodologies would need to be developed. It should be concerned more with rationing and its effects and with 'damage analysis' in the long term. He suggests that new forms of analysis are needed, which would expose who benefits from a policy, which groups and which areas;

expose the authority's present rationing system and how it works; help to understand the constraints that limit policy changes as opposed to the myths that are believed to limit them; and, finally, provide the 'imaginative leap' that sees new possibilities in the use of old resources. He concludes:

> If in these and many other ways corporate planning can find ways of guiding local authorities to growth in achievement in a no growth situation, it will have achieved its purpose. If corporate planning remains geared to the methodologies of growth, then it will soon be forgotten. Above all, this is no time to retreat from corporate planning. The time has come to pursue it in a new form. The choice is there for local government to make.
>
> (p. 20)

This is not a radical argument for a centralized system of decision-making but a plea for a strengthened reformist element which will analyse, challenge and guide. Through this process the pressure will be kept on the professional departments to review their own position and to seek creative solutions either within their own service or jointly with others.

The departments do not lose their autonomy. To do so would mean the loss of a great deal. Expertise, norms and values established over time contain much that is necessary and valuable. The argument from the profession is a necessary check on over-enthusiastic reform, however imaginative and novel the solutions proposed by the reformers may seem at first sight.

The professions thus take on the role of defenders: a crucial role in a time of persistent cuts. Change is necessary, but not unbridled ill-considered change. The opposing forces of defensiveness and reformism provide essential checks upon each other.

It is interesting to note that Walsh *et al.* (1984) conclude their study of the management of falling rolls with the notion of balance between schools and their local authorities:

If the problems of the future are to be met then innovation must be possible in a period of contraction as well as one of growth. Both schools and authorities will need to be able to work together as problem solvers and there will need to be both centralization and decentralization at the same time. Centrally the authorities will be needed to coordinate the work of different and varying institutions, to enable them to work together and to enable the student to find the most appropriate provision within the system. Schools will need to be less jealous of their autonomy and internally more participative. The authority's appropriate role is one of making it possible for schools to develop by setting the boundaries of development and the framework within which development can succeed.

(p. 281)

The same 'central–decentral' balance should also be created or re-created between central and local government and, within local government, between corporate management and departments which would maintain much of their traditional autonomy. The resulting process will not look tidy. There will always be major conflicts of interest and uncertainties. The resulting culture of choice will not be a convivial situation in which to work and will place heavy demands on its officials and members. But the alternatives in the long term may be less attractive.

That change has to occur is not in doubt, and indeed many of the measures proposed by the government are regarded by those within the profession as important and necessary. The problem, at and between all levels, is how to bring about major changes in a way that preserves what is best within the system.

The main danger in a cuts culture is remaining too reactionary and not providing the policy space in which the 'imaginative leap' can take place. In education, external circumstances may force change to take place, but those having internal control of the system have a responsibility to see that they bring to bear, on that change, their accumulated professional judgement. The dilemma for the organization is to achieve the right balance. To capitulate to external pressures without defence is to lose much of potential value; whilst to engage entirely in defensiveness, without admitting the need for reform, may mean that the solution that is finally imposed by those who hold the power will be good for nobody. As Klein (1973) points out:

> To ignore that which is being defended may mean that the planned change itself is flawed; it may also mean that the process of change becomes transformed into a conflict situation in which forces struggle in opposition and in which energies become increasingly devoted to winning rather than to solving the original problem.
>
> (p. 120)

In order to create a future that encourages and facilitates imaginative change, the reformist element within the culture certainly has to be preserved and strengthened. This has already happened, to some extent by default, in the crisis culture. Power has shifted, naturally, to those outside of the service departments in order to deal quickly with threats to the organizations' survival. In the balanced culture advocated here, however, this power would remain but would be controlled and used creatively and sensitively. Reformers would accept the necessity of informed opposition. The nature of the different tasks of the reformers and defenders would be recognized; so would their separate contributions in a time of contraction. What is advocated is a difficult middle course that pulls together the best of the reformist and defensive elements of the culture. Those who practise the art carry a heavy responsibility for the future.

The future for education will almost certainly continue to be challenging. Local education authorities will find, as they have already, that a central government is prepared to impose solutions and create its own policy space.

There also seems little doubt that either prolonged crisis or the possibility of a cuts culture are the main alternatives that will have to be accepted. If that is the case, then those in local government, and particularly in education, will do well to study the art of defence as well as reform and pragmatism.

The greatest task of all, though, and perhaps the best defence in the long run, will be the art of combining them creatively in order to maintain local government in reasonable shape during a continuing period of contraction and recession.

As a postscript, and as an indication that the problems of recession are likely to remain for some time, a few of the main headlines from *The Times Educational Supplement* of 26 April 1985 are quoted. They make sobering reading:

Seere 'cash penalties' for l.e.a.s meeting 3% pay award.

(p. 1)

More posts to go.

(p. 1)

Why education badly needs a change of Act (R. A. Butler).

(p. 4)

An increasing number of l.e.a.s are now coming to heel on the Government's spending plans.

(p. 12)

Cash penalties force 4 in 5 l.e.a.s to plan further real cuts in budgets.

(p. 12)

Less spent on upkeep [of schools].

(p. 12)

110,400 places to go.

(p. 12)

Capitation failing to match inflation.

(p. 13)

Reinforcing this gloomy picture is the report by Her Majesty's Inspectors published in May 1985 (HMI, 1985). Two short extracts will illustrate the concern felt by the Inspectorate:

The most serious state of affairs is the deteriorating quality and appropriateness of the accommodation in which pupils learn and teachers and lecturers work . . . Much of the nation's school building stock is now below acceptable standard . . .

(p. 8)

While both AFE and NAFE [advanced and non advanced further education] are better provided for and more buoyant, it does appear that the cumulative effects of coping in this way are making themselves felt in the schools. Many are unable to replace dilapidated and outdated sets of books and equipment; to carry out the many curricular developments needed across the 5 to 16 and 16 to 19 age ranges; and to respond to the planned and desired new developments such as the GCSE, CPVE and AS level examinations, and records of achievement. In all this, the quality and commitment of teachers are vital if success is to be achieved. But good teaching can neither be nurtured nor sustained where resources are inadequate in quality and quantity; where rooms are shabby and in need of repair; and where the time for planning, development and in-service training is insufficient.

(p. 9)

And yet against this background of a 'starving' educational system there are new resources available, and because the system desperately needs extra money this additional 'bait' is much sought after whatever its source and whatever conditions are attached to its use. Large sums are available from or through the Department of Education and Science, the Manpower Services Committee and the European Community but these grants have to be applied for and used for specific purposes. For instance DES circular 3/85 refers to a sum of £10.8 million to be 'made available to authorities for the period 1.9.85 to 31.8.86 in respect of school teachers released for eligible courses in priority areas'. A letter from the MSC to local authorities refers to a sum of £25 million for a new in-service training scheme 'to promote developments across the curriculum as a whole of the kind the government has sought to encourage through, in particular, TVEI.'

For many local authorities these new monies are providing an increasing proportion of their budget, sometimes between 5 and 10 per cent. Given that about 90 per cent of their normal budgets are tied to relatively fixed items such as teachers' pay, overheads etc., these new grants represent a major new dimension in the financing and control of local education.

Education is still in recession and is changing rapidly. To a very large extent that change is being imposed from the centre. Whether those changes will eventually improve the service remains to be seen but it is clear that local education authorities, traditionally the providers of education within their locality, are now much less in control of events. Although many changes may have an underlying political or ideological motivation it is the cuts themselves and the power over resources which have provided the circumstances conducive to their implementation.

Beware: *Education in recession can be dangerous!*

Appendix: Some Methodological Issues

There are two important issues which influence research of the kind described in this book and affect what is done, how it is done and how it is reported. They are 'perspective' and 'approach' and they are dealt with in turn.

Perspective

A key issue in the social sciences relates to the problem of objectivity versus subjectivity. It is possible to approach the study of an organization, or its policy-making procedures, in one of two distinct ways.

In one, the researcher holds certain preconceived ideas which usually take the form of a set of related concepts giving structure and direction to the research. In studying an organization, for instance, concepts such as power, authority, value, system, role, bureaucracy or corporate structure might be used. The research might involve an attempt to refine a definition of power, or to establish a connection between, say, the number of administrators and the size of an organization.

This perspective is based on the view that there is a real social world which can be identified, observed and measured. It exists independently of any individual who forms part of it. Such a view leads to methods of research akin to those used in the natural sciences, including, for instance, hypothesis formation, experimental testing and quantitative techniques of data gathering and analysis.

Opposed to this perspective is the form of research that regards organizations, and all forms of social life, as no more than the product of individual and shared meanings generated by those involved. A researcher entering the field with this perspective would attempt to suspend his or her own knowledge and beliefs in order to 'hear' as clearly as possible the messages and meanings conveyed by the participants. He or she would not use externally generated concepts, models and theories but would, instead, try to provide the opportunity for the nature and characteristics of the situation to unfold during the course of the inquiry.

The researcher would use techniques such as participant observation, non-directive interviews and the analysis of the language of those involved.

The two camps – objective and subjective – present distinct views on the nature of organizations and the ways in which they can and should be studied. Proponents of either view find it difficult to accept the value of work carried out by the other. So is there a tenable middle ground?

The kind of research which seeks to bridge the gap between the two standpoints comes under attack from both sides. Research in this area is regarded by the objective purists as woolly and unscientific and by those adopting a subjective stance as too concerned with essentially artificial theoretical concepts far removed from the day-to-day realities of the actors in the situation.

To hold the middle ground means accepting that both objective and subjective viewpoints are important in interpreting a social situation. The 'reality' envisaged from this standpoint couples organization conditions, which can be described using terms such as 'structure', 'hierarchy' and 'authority', with the subjective meanings, individual or shared, which those who form the social group use to make sense of their world. These participants are neither the product of their situation nor entirely free agents within it – they interact, negotiate and have some influence on the groups and organization of which they are a part.

The roots of this intermediate position can be traced back to Max Weber, who was dissatisfied with the superficialities which he regarded as characterizing positivistic explanations of society but was also concerned with the overly subjective and unscientific nature of idealist thought. His writings on this subject suggested the possibility of a hybrid position which was later developed by other writers such as Goffman (1961), Berger and Luckmann (1964), Silverman and Jones (1976), Day and Day (1977) and Strauss (1978).

A useful illustration of the position is provided by Day and Day (1977) in their explanation of negotiated order:

> In the case of negotiated order theory, the individuals in organisations play an active, self-conscious role in the shaping of social order. Their day-to-day interaction, agreements, temporary refusals, and changing definitions of the situations at hand are of paramount importance. Closely correlated is the perspective's view of social reality . . . the negotiated order theory down-plays the notion of organisations as fixed, rather rigid systems which are highly constrained by strict rules, regulations and goals and hierarchical chains of command. Instead, it emphasises the fluid, continuously emerging qualities of the organisation, the changing web of interaction woven among its members, and it suggests that order is something at which members of the organisation must consistently work.
>
> (p. 132)

Although this explanation is related to the notion of 'negotiated order' it is equally applicable to other issues, such as how policy is made and implemented, or how priorities are ordered and conflicts resolved. The idea of fluidity and a 'changing web of interaction' amongst participants, seen against a background of semi-permanent structural features, is an important one in this approach. As Strauss (1978) puts it:

> nobody espousing a negotiated order perspective has ever ignored structural considerations, has ever taken over uncritically the constructed world of the actors under study. In any event the paradigmatic certainly takes both actor's viewpoints and structural considerations into account.
>
> (p. 251)

What form will a report based upon this middle ground take? Combining objective and subjective standpoints will surely place the researcher in a judgemental position and demand interpretations of events and situations which themselves rely upon the researchers own subjective view. A report which says 'this is how it is', by interpreting the relationship between structural factors and the subjective meanings, values and perspectives of the participants, places upon the researcher a considerable onus of responsibility.

However, this responsibility is no more than that faced by those occupying the more extreme objective or subjective perspectives. The former face the problem of justifying their externally generated theoretical perspective; and the latter, the problem of ensuring that the views of the participants are clearly understood and presented in an unbiased way.

Those taking the middle ground, and this includes the present author, face problems of the same methodological order as those in the other two 'camps' in defending their position. Their interpretive stance must rely for its validation upon an acceptance of its findings by an appropriate audience – a point which is taken up again in connection with the case study approach dealt with next.

Approach

The approach adopted in this research is to take a 'case study' as the basis of the work but to combine this with the broader picture. As was said in the introduction, the 'story' is woven from the strands of three levels of analysis – national, local and schools – and moves back and forth between the three using each one to illustrate the others. But underlying and grounding the whole research is the case study.

Kenny and Grotelueschen (1984) define case study as, typically, 'intensive investigations of single cases which serve both to identify and describe basic phenomena, as well as provide the basis for subsequent theory-development' (p. 37). Both points need some elaboration. What is a case, and how might case study lead to 'theory development'?

Stake (1978) suggests that a case can be whatever 'bounded system is of interest'. An institution, a programme, a responsibility, a collection, or a population can all be a case. The boundary, which provides the focus, need not be closed; indeed, the idea of permeable boundaries is generally more acceptable in so far as the case can then more easily be related to its context.

Guba and Lincoln (1981) define three types of case study which they call 'factual', 'interpretive' and 'evaluative' (p. 374). The factual, they maintain, will generally 'record, construct, present and examine' and will produce a 'register, profile, cognitions and facts'. The interpretive will tend to 'construe, synthesize, clarify, and relate' and produce 'history, meanings, understandings and theory'. Finally, the evaluative type will 'deliberate, epitomize, contrast, and weigh' and produce 'evidence, portrayals, discriminations and judgements'.

The present study is largely 'interpretive' although with some elements of the 'evaluative'. It examines policy-making in one local education authority with a view to providing a greater understanding of the process through a historical analysis and the clarification of key structures, values, meanings and contextual factors within and surrounding the case. It also aims to provide theoretical insights, and this leads to the next point.

Theory Construction

Ribbins and Brown (1979), discussing case studies of secondary school reorganization, make the point that most studies are primarily descriptive, empirical and specific in character. They continue:

> Although there is usually some analysis of the case study itself there is, for the most part, little attempt to relate the study to other similar studies of the reorganisation of secondary education, let alone to case studies in other areas of

education or to theories of local government generally. In short, rarely do such studies attempt to yield or to test propositions that seem applicable beyond the confines of their particular circumstances.

(p. 189)

Heclo (1974), reviewing developments in policy analysis, considers that there is a great untapped potential in the use of case study to produce theoretical perspectives. He goes on to suggest that without such perspectives the study will be 'at best an interesting contribution to historical scholarship and at worst an uninteresting, episodic narrative'. However, he continues: 'There appears to be nothing about the case study technique which is inherently nontheoretical or unscientific; the problem lies in assuming that the theoretical contributions will emerge automatically from narrative' (p. 93).

Heclo notes the problem of attempting to generalize from specific actions to the performance of whole systems but argues that this can be overcome. He cites as an example Glenn Paige's analysis of decisions leading to United States intervention in Korea and how the author was able to 'systematically derive interesting generalisations concerning the effect of crisis on organisational, informational, and evaluative variables'.

Adelman, Kemmis and Jenkins (1980) argue that as the study progresses the boundaries of the case appear increasingly permeable and problematic. The issues which arise in the apparently unique situation of the case are soon seen to be embedded in real world situations. As such they are recognizable as general problems which have wider significance. The case study invites the reader 'to underwrite the account by appealing to his tacit knowledge of human situations'.

Stake (1980) makes a similar point when he speaks of 'naturalistic generalization, arrived at by recognizing the natural covariations of happenings'. Such generalizations are valuable in the sense that they ring true to the reader, who recognizes the issue, problem, idea, or hypothesis as one which, although generated from one particular situation, applies to other situations of which he or she is aware.

The processes of investigation and hypothesizing which lead to the formulation of generalized ideas are not unlike the formulation of 'grounded theory' as described by Glaser and Strauss (1975). They comment:

> To generate theories . . . we suggest as the best approach an initial systematic discovery of theory from the data of social research. Then one can be relatively sure that the theory will fit and work. And since the categories are discovered by examination of the data, laymen involved in the area to which the theory applies will usually be able to understand it, while sociologists who work in other areas will recognise an understandable theory linked with the data of a given area.
>
> (p. 4)

This is an important point. It concerns the validity of the interpretive or evaluative case study approach and its place amongst other forms of social research. To a large extent it relies for its effectiveness upon its ability to convey meaningful information to the reader – whether layman or specialist. It must be understandable to both, and the findings and ideas which emerge must seem reasonable and acceptable to those the study seeks to inform.

Furthermore, case study, as a result of its relative freedom from dogmatic methodological constraints, can afford flexibility in the choice of research tools. Heclo (1974) stresses this advantage:

> a second facet of their potential usefulness is the richness and flexibility of analysis which is available in case studies. In terms of technical tools, the approach can integrate existing historical studies, secondary sources, aggregate quantitative data, participant interviews and sample surveys. Correspondingly, in terms of analytic depth, policy case studies have at least the potential for encompassing and bringing to bear a remarkable variety of factors – from individual motivations and perceptions to comprehensive socio-economic movements . . . To be sure, there is no agreed format for

integrating the variety of quantitative and qualitative factors effectively in play, but this should not obscure the fact that the richness of case studies promises to be more faithful to the complexity of modern policies than might otherwise be the case.

(pp. 94–5)

Advantage was taken of this potential richness of approach in the present study, and the range of methods used is described next.

Research Methods Used

Over a period of three years (1981–4) regular visits were made to Shire; some for a day, others for two weeks, depending upon the nature of the work. During this time over ninety interviews were conducted, and thirty meetings observed including education committee, policy and resources, the county council and certain corporate groups. Eighteen councillors representing all political parties and mainly members of the education committee were interviewed, together with four added members on the committee. The councillors included: Chairman and Deputy Chairman of Council, Chairman and Deputy Chairman of Education and the leaders of the three political parties.

Interviews were also held with twenty-five officers, some on several occasions, including: the Chief Executive, Chief and Deputy Chief Education Officers, County Treasurer and County Secretary. Free access was given to a wide range of documents at Shire Hall, and a great deal of the evidence was collected from analysis of reports, minutes and statistical records.

Visits were made to sixteen schools, and the heads, deputy heads and some senior teachers were interviewed. These visits were followed by a questionnaire to all heads in the county regarding the effects of the cuts. Data obtained from this source was later analysed by computer.

Interviews were also held with officials at the Department

of Education and Science and at the party headquarters of the Conservative and Labour parties.

The development of a wider theoretical perspective was related not only to the evidence obtained from the field study, but also to the considerable amount of information available nationally regarding local authority policy-making. This, in itself, can be seen as part of a much wider context of relevant literature on such topics as the study of organizations, policy analysis, evaluation and economics. These external sources were all used to expand the focus of the study to more general issues.

As the study progressed, parts of the report were written in draft form and used as the basis for discussion with officers, singly or in groups.

By the end of the fieldwork the amount of data was considerable. The problem mentioned by Heclo (1974) of finding a format for the integration of the quantitative and qualitative factors had to be resolved. There were various possible solutions to this problem which depended, in this case, upon how policy was to be defined and upon the specific purpose of the study. For instance, a narrow definition of policy, concerning only the actual process of negotiation and coupled with an interest in, say, party political influences on policy, would produce one kind of study. An interest in, say, the costs and benefits of particular policies would produce quite a different result.

In this study, policy is taken in its broadest form. In essence it represents the 'broad plans, general principles, and priorities from which programs stem' (Cronbach *et al.*, 1980, p. 101). But the focus was always on the problem of recession. The original research questions were concerned with this, the fieldwork concentrated upon it, and much of the questioning and discussions revolved around this and associated issues.

Given a broad definition of policy, a specific concern with contraction and, most importantly, the emergence of certain key ideas concerning 'cultures of choice', it seemed sensible to present the report as a portrayal of different kinds of policy milieu. These, as it happened, seemed to follow one another over time. The first two, *laissez-faire* and planned growth, provided an historical background; the crisis culture portrayed the ongoing situation for Shire and many other authorities; finally, the cuts culture, although still only emerging, projected the study into the future.

This 'four culture' format thus provided not only a case study of one situation but also a means whereby the evidence from one specific example could be related to more general issues and concerns thereby overcoming the narrowness criticized by Ribbins and Brown (1979).

References

Adelman, C., Kemmis, S. and Jenkins, D. (1980), 'Rethinking case study: notes from the second Cambridge conference', in H. Simons (ed.), *Towards a Science of the Singular* (University of East Anglia: Centre for Applied Educational Research).

Bains, M. A. (1972), *The New Local Authorities: Management Structure, Report of a Study Group* (London: HMSO).

Berg, B. and Östergren, B. (1977), *Innovations and Innovation Processes in Higher Education* (Stockholm: National Board of Universities and Colleges [ÜHA]).

Berger, P. L. and Luckmann, T. (1971), *The Social Construction of Reality* (Harmondsworth: Penguin).

Billings, R. S., Milburn, T. W. and Schaalman, M. L. (1980), 'A model of crisis perception: a theoretical and empirical analysis', *Administrative Science Quarterly*, vol. 25, June 1980, pp. 300–16.

Blaug, M. (1970), *Economics of Education, a Selected Annotated Bibliography*, 2nd edn (Oxford: Pergamon).

Braybrooke, D. and Lindblom, C. E. (1970), *A Strategy of Decision: Policy Evaluation as a Social Process* (London: Collier Macmillan).

Burgess, T. (1983), *Financial Management in Schools: The Cambridgeshire Scheme 1982–83*, Working Paper on Institutions (London: North East London Polytechnic).

Burrell, G. and Morgan, G. (1978), *Sociological Paradigms and Organizational Analysis* (London: Heinemann).

Bush, T. and Kogan, M. (1982), *Directors of Education* (London: Allen & Unwin).

Caldicott, P. J. (1985), 'Organizational causes of stress', *Educational Management and Administration*, vol. 13, no. 2, Summer 1985, pp. 90–3.

Carley, M. (1980), *Rational Techniques in Policy Analysis* (London: Heinemann).

Carron and Williams (1985) (London: Allen & Unwin).

Carter, J. (1981), *Day Services for Adults: Somewhere to Go*, National Institute Social Services Library No. 40 (London: Allen & Unwin).

Castling, A. (1983), 'Staff development: a case study on stress', in G. Squires (ed.), *Innovation Through Recession* (Guildford: Society for Research into Higher Education).

Caulcott, T. (1983), 'Responding to the challenge: the public sector in recession', *Local Government Studies*, vol. 9, no. 6, November 1983, pp. 69–85.

181

CBI (1979), *Value for Money*. Report on Cheshire County Council carried out by P. A. Management Consultants (Manchester Confederation of British Industry).

CCCS (1981), *Unpopular Education: Schooling and Social Democracy in England since 1944*, Education Group, Centre for Contemporary Cultural Studies, University of Birmingham (London: Hutchinson).

CIPFA (1984), *Education Statistics*, constant price ready reckoner (London: Chartered Institute of Public Finance and Accountancy).

Cronbach, L. J. *et al.* (1980), *Towards Reform of Program Evaluation* (San Francisco: Jossey Bass).

CSO (1973), *National Income and Expenditure 1962–1973*, Section 1, Central Statistical Office (London: HMSO).

Cyert, C. M. (1978), 'The management of universities of constant or decreasing size', *Public Administration Review*, July/August 1978, pp. 344–9.

Day, R. and Day, J. (1977), 'A review of the current state of negotiated order theory', *Sociological Quarterly*, 18, pp. 126–42.

DES (1970), *Output Budgeting for the Department of Education and Science* (London: HMSO).

DES (1973), *Statistics of Education 5, Finance and Awards* (London: HMSO).

DES (1982), *Handbook of Unit Costs* (London: DES).

DES (1983), *Annual Report* (London: HMSO).

DES (1983a), *Statistical Bulletin*, 10/83 (London: DES).

DES (1984), *Statistics of Education: Schools 1983* (London: DES).

DES (1985), *Better Schools*, Cmnd 9469 (London: HMSO).

DOE (1980), *Grant Related Expenditure. How the Expenditure Needs of Local Authorities are Assessed in the New Block Grant* (London: Department of the Environment).

Douglas, J. W. B. (1964), *The Home and the School: A Study of Ability Attainment in the Primary School* (London: Panther).

Eddison, T. (1975), *Local Government: Management and Corporate Planning* (Leighton Buzzard: Leonard Hill).

Else, P. K. and Marshall, G. P. (1981), 'The unplanning of public expenditure: recent problems of expenditure planning and the consequences of cash limits', *Public Administration*, vol. 59, autumn 1981, pp. 253–78.

FEU (1984), *Towards a Competence-Based System: An FEU View* (London: Further Education Unit, DES).

Fletcher, C. (1980), 'Developments in community education: a current account', in C. Fletcher and N. Thompson, op. cit.

Fletcher, C. and Thompson, N. (1980), *Issues in Community Education* (Lewes: Falmer Press).

Fletcher, C., Maxine, C. and Williams, W. (1985), *Schools on Trial* (Milton Keynes: Open University Press).

Floud, J., Halsey, A. H. and Anderson, C. A. (1961), *Economy and Society: A Reader in the Sociology of Education* (London: Macmillan).

Freire, P. (1972), *Pedagogy of the Oppressed* (Harmondsworth: Penguin).

Gibson, J. F. (1982), 'The block (and target) grant system and local authority expenditure – theory and evidence', *Local Government Studies*, vol. 8, no. 3, May/June 1982, pp. 15–31.

Glaser, B. G. and Strauss, A. (1975), *Towards a Grounded Theory* (Chicago: Aldine).

Glassberg, A. (1978), 'Organizational responses to municipal budget decreases', *Public Administration Review*, vol. 38, July/August 1978, pp. 325–31.

Goffman, E. (1961), *Asylums: Essays on the Social Situation of Patients and Other Inmates* (New York: Doubleday).

Goodman, P. (1971), *Compulsory Miseducation* (Harmondsworth: Penguin).

Greenwood, R. (1983), Changing patterns of budgeting in English local government', *Public Administration*, vol. 61, summer 1983, pp. 149–68.

Greenwood, R. *et al.* (1976), *In Pursuit of Corporate Rationality* (University of Birmingham: Institute of Local Government Studies).

Guba, E. G. and Lincoln, Y. S. (1981), *Effective Evaluation* (San Francisco: Jossey Bass).

Gyford, J. and James, M. (1982), *Party Political Linkages between Centre and Locality*, A report to the Social Science Research Council (London: University College).

Habermas, J. (1976), *Legitimation Crisis*, trans. T. McCarthy (London: Heinemann).

Handy, C. (1976), *Understanding Organizations* (Harmondsworth: Penguin).

Hargreaves, D. H. (1967), *Social Relations in the Secondary School* (London: Routledge & Kegan Paul).

Heclo, H. H. (1974), 'Review article: policy analysis', *British Journal of Political Science*, vol. 2, pp. 83–108.

Herman, C. F. (ed) (1972) *International Crises*: Insights from behavioral research. N. Y. Free Press.

Hickson, P. J. *et al.* (1973), 'A strategic contingencies theory of intra-organisational power', in G. Salaman and K. Thompson (eds.), *People and Organisations* (London: Longman).

Hinings, R. *et al.* (1980), *Management Systems in Local Government* (University of Birmingham: Institute of Local Government Studies).

HMI (1981), *Report by HMI on the Effects on the Education Service in England of Local Authority Expenditure Policies – Financial Year 1980–81* (London: DES).

HMI (1982), *Report by HMI . . . 1981–82* (as above) (London: DES).

HMI (1983), *Report by HMI . . . 1982–3* (as above) (London: DES).

HMI (1985), *Report by HMI . . . 1984–5* (as above) (London: DES).

Holt, J. (1971), *The Underachieving School* (Harmondsworth: Penguin).

Humphrey, C. and Thomas, H. (1983), 'Making effective use of scarce resources', *Education*, 12 August.

Illich, I. (1971), *Deschooling Society* (New York: Doubleday).

ILEA (1984), *Improving Secondary Schools*, Report of the Committee of the Curriculum and Organization of Secondary Schools, The Hargreaves Report (London: ILEA).

Jackson, R. J. (1976), 'Crisis management and policy making: an exploration of theory and research', in R. Rose (ed.), *The Dynamics of Public Policy* (London: Sage).

Jenkins, W. I. (1978), *Policy Analysis: A Political and Organizational Perspective* (London: Martin Robertson).

Jennings, R. E. (1977), *Education and Politics: Policy-Making in Local Education Authorities* (London: Batsford).

Jones, K., Brown, J. and Bradshaw, J. (1983), *Issues in Social Policy* (London: Routledge & Kegan Paul).

Kemp, R. L. (1983), 'More on managing in hard times', *Local Government Studies*, vol. 9, no. 6, pp. 1–6.

Kenny, W. R. and Grotelueschen, A. D. (1984), 'Making the case for case study', *Journal of Curriculum Studies*, vol. 16.1, pp. 37–51.

King, R. D., Raynes, N. V. and Tizzard, J. (1971), *Patterns of Residential Care: Sociological Studies in Institutions for Handicapped Children* (London: Routledge).

Kirst, M. W. (1977), 'What happens at local level after school finance reform', *Policy Studies 1977*, no. 3, pp. 303–24.

Klein, D. (1973), 'Some notes on the dynamics of resistance to change: the defender role', in W. G. Bennis, K. D. Benne and R. Chin, *The Planning of Change*, 2nd edn (London: Holt, Rinehart & Winston).

Kogan, M. (1975), *Educational Policy Making: A Study of Interest Groups and Parliament* (London: Allen & Unwin).

Kozol, J. (1971), *Death at an Early Age* (Harmondsworth: Penguin).

Lacey, C. (1970), *Hightown Grammar: The School as a Social System* (Manchester: Manchester University Press).

Levine, C. H. (1978), 'Organizational decline and cutback management', *Public Administration Review*, vol. 38, July/August 1978, pp. 316–24.

Lord, R. (1983), 'Value for money in the education service', *Public Money*, vol. 3, no. 2, September 1983, pp. 15–22.

Mackenzie, K. D. (1978), *Organizational Structures* (Arlington Heights, Ill.: AHM).

Mann, J. (1979), *Education* (London: Pitman).

Manning, A. J., Mercer, R. H. and Whiting, N. E. (1982), *Contraction Management in Schools and Colleges: an annotated bibliography* (Sheffield City Polytechnic: Department of Education Management).

March, J. G. and Olsen, J. P. (1976), *Ambiguity and Choice in Organisations* (New York: Wiley).

Maud, Sir John (later Lord Redcliffe-Maude) (1967), *Management of Local Government: Report of the Committee*, five vols. (London: HMSO).

Michels, R. (1962), *Political Parties: A Sociological Study of the Oligarchical Tendencies of Modern Democracy* (New York: Free Press).

Miller, E. J. and Gwynne, G. V. (1972), *A Life Apart: A Pilot Study of Residential Institutions for the Physically Handicapped and the Young Chronic Sick* (London: Tavistock).

Morris, P. (1969), *Put Away: A Sociological Study of Institutions for the Mentally Retarded* (London: Routledge & Kegan Paul).

NAS/UWT (1983), *Cuts in the Education Service: A Survey* (Birmingham: National Association of Schoolmasters and Union of Women Teachers).

Newsom (1963) *Half Our Future*, The Newsom Report (London: HMSO).

Noble, T. and Pym, B. (1970), 'Collegial authority and the receding locus of power', *British Journal of Sociology*, vol. 21, pp. 431–51.

NUT (1982), *Schools Speak Out. The effects of expenditure cuts on primary education* (London: National Union of Teachers).

NUT (1983), *Manifesto for Education* (London: National Union of Teachers).

Penrose, E. (1959), *The Theory of the Growth of the Firm* (London: Blackwell).

Pettigrew, A. M. (1983), 'Patterns of managerial response as organisations move from rich to poor environments', *Educational Management and Administration*, vol. 11, no. 2, pp. 98–104.

Pfeffer, J. (1982), *Organizations and Organization Theory* (Boston: Pitman).

Plowden (1967), *Children and Their Primary Schools*, the Plowden Report (London: HMSO).

Postman, N. and Weingartner, C. (1971), *Teaching as a Subversive Activity* (Harmondsworth: Penguin).

Poster, C. (1982), *Community Development: Its Development and Management* (London: Heinemann).

Regan, D. E. (1977), *Local Government and Education* (London: Allen & Unwin).

Reimer, E. (1971), *School is Dead* (Harmondsworth: Penguin).

Ribbins, P. M. and Brown, R. J. (1979), 'Policy making in English local government: the case of secondary reorganisation', *Public Administration*, vol. 57, pp. 187–202.

Ridley, F. F. (1972), 'Public administration: cause for discontent', *Public Administration*, vol. 50, spring 1972, pp. 65–85.

Robbins (1963), *Higher Education*, the Robbins Report (London: HMSO).

RSA (1984), 'Education for capability', *Newsletter*, autumn 1984 (London: Royal Society of Arts).

SEO (1974), *Management in the Education Service: Challenge and Response*, Society of Education Officers (London: Routledge & Kegan Paul).

Silver, H. (1980), *Education and the Social Condition* (London: Methuen).

Silverman, D. and Jones, J. (1976), *Organizational Work: The Language of Grading/The Grading of Language* (London and New York: Collier Macmillan).

Simon, H. A., Smithberg, D. W. and Thompson, V. A. (1950), *Public Administration* (New York: Knopf).

Spencer, K. (1984), 'Assessing alternative forms of service provision', *Local Government Studies*, vol. 10, no. 2, pp. 14–20.

Spiers, M. (1975), *Techniques and Public Administration: A Contextual Evaluation* (London: Fontana).

Stake, R. E. (1978), 'The case study method in social inquiry', *Educational Researcher*, vol. 7, pp. 5–8.

Stake, R. E. (1980), 'The case study method in social inquiry', in H. Simons, (ed.), *Towards a Science of the Singular* (University of East Anglia: Centre for Applied Educational Research).

Stewart, J. D. (1977), *Management in an Era of Restraint and Central and Local Government Relationships* (London: Municipal Group).

Stewart, J. D. (1983), 'Recipe for irresponsibility', *The Times Educational Supplement*, 12 August 1983.

Stewart, J. D. (1983a), *Local Government: The Conditions of Local Choice* (London: Allen & Unwin).

Strauss, A. (1978), *Negotiations* (San Francisco: Jossey Bass).

Taylor, L. C. (1971), *Resources for Learning* (Harmondsworth: Penguin).

TES (1985), LEA spending survey, *The Times Educational Supplement*, 26 April 1985, pp. 12–13.

Townsend, P. (1962), *The Last Refuge: A Survey of Residential Institutions and Homes for the Aged in England and Wales* (London: Routledge & Kegan Paul).

Travers, T. (1983), 'Plotting the rise and fall of GRE's', *Education*, 29 April 1983, p. 332.

Vaizey, J. (1962), *Education for Tomorrow: Britain in the Sixties* (Harmondsworth: Penguin).

Vaizey, J. and Sheenan, J. (1968), *Resources for Education* (London: Allen & Unwin).

Walsh, K., *et al.* (1982), *The Management of Teachers: Problems of Contraction* (Birmingham University: Institute of Local Government Studies).

Walsh, K., *et al.* (1983), *Falling School Rolls and the Management of the Teaching Profession* (Birmingham University: Institute of Local Government Studies).

Walsh, K., *et al.* (1984), *Falling School Rolls and the Management of the Teaching Profession* (Windsor: NFER/Nelson).

Wilson, S. (1980), 'The school and the community', in C. Fletcher and N. Thompson (eds.), *Issues in Community Education* (Lewes: Falmer Press).

Young, Lord (1984), *The Technical and Vocational Educational Initiative*, Head Teacher's Review, winter 1984, pp. 8–10.

Index

187

R